TEXAS WILDFLOWERS

TEXAS WILDFLOWERS

Photographs by Leo Meier

Text by Jan Reid

Botanical consultant: Geyata Ajilvsgi

PORTLAND HOUSE
New York

Produced by Weldon Owen Pty Limited
43 Victoria Street McMahons Point
NSW 2060, Australia
Telex AA23038; Fax (02) 929 8352
A member of the Weldon International Group of Companies
Sydney • Hong Kong • London • Chicago • San Francisco

Publisher: John Owen
Publishing Manager: Stuart Laurence
Project Coordinator: Jane Fraser
Senior Editor: Derek Barton
Editor: Jean Hardy
Captions: Geyata Ajilusgi

Designer: John Bull, The Book Design Company
Map: Stan Lamond, The Book Design Company

A Weldon Owen Production

First published in 1989
©Copyright 1989 News America Publishing Corporation Inc,
and Weldon Owen Publishing Limited.
This 1990 edition published by Portland House
distributed by Outlet Book Company, Inc.,
a Random House Company,
225 Park Avenue South, New York, N.Y. 10003

ISBN 0-517-05059-5
87654321

Typesetting: Authentic Print and Amazing Faces, Sydney, Australia
Printed by Kyodo Printing Company
Printed and bound in Singapore

Pages 2-3:
Dew of early morning adds a freshness and sparkle to
cut-leaved evening primrose.
Page 5:
A mosaic of lemon-mint, Indian blanket, and cornflower
exhibits its gay colors in the termperamental winds of early spring.
Pages 6-7:
Tall and stately, century plants reach skyward against a
backdrop of craggy mountains.

PREFACE

⚜

*I*n Texas, sky is the constant — sky and distance and color. With over 2,500 wildflower species, Texas has been known for its extravagant floral panoramas since it was roamed by nomadic Indian tribes and French and Spanish explorers. Wildflowers thrive in communion with grasses, and virgin Texas was more than seventy percent prairie. The continued abundance of blossoming plants reflects the range and contrast of the contemporary Texas landscape: from the Gulf Coast's barrier islands to craggy Rocky Mountain peaks, from the rain forests of East Texas to far West Texas's bone-dry share of the Chihuahuan Desert.

Each region of this diverse state has its own special wildflowers, and they have adapted wonderfully to the exigencies of climate and soil. Delicate wild orchids, vines, and ferns thrive in the Big Thicket of East Texas; flesh-eating plants capture insects in swamps and bogs. On the barrier islands and in desert West Texas, wind-driven sand dunes are stabilized by the roots of wildflowers. When spring comes to the North Texas plains, severe and sparsely featured terrain suddenly leaps with color. Wildflowers bloom year-round in the subtropical Rio Grande Valley. Plants of the rugged Trans-Pecos accept the terms of withering sun and scarce water. During the heat of the day, bristling cactus open the desert's loveliest blooms.

In text and photographs, *Texas Wildflowers* is an exploration of the state's natural heritage and a celebration of its varied floral beauty.

Clumps of Indian blanket are softly back-lit by the sun's first rays.

Overleaf: From earliest spring to late summer, Indian blanket (also called "firewheel" and "gaillardia") sets the roadsides ablaze with brilliant blossoms.

PHOTO: STEPHAN MYERS

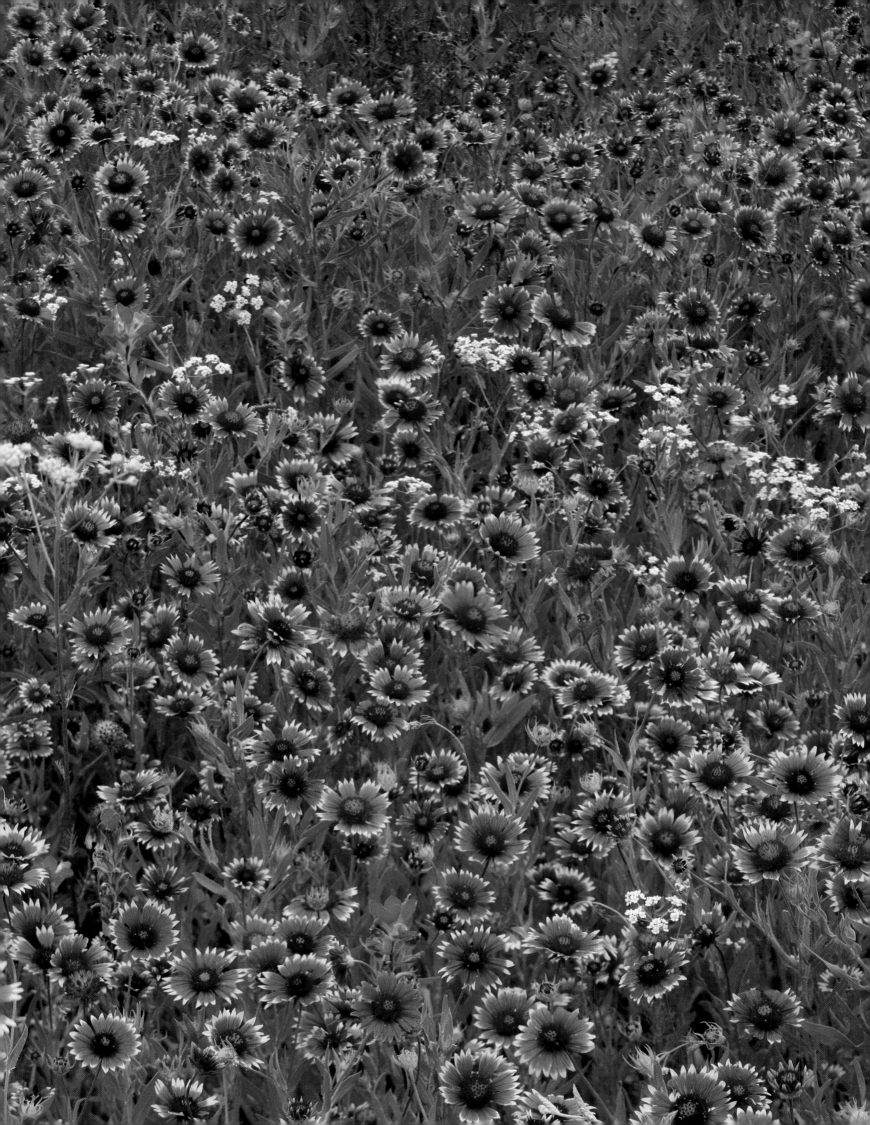

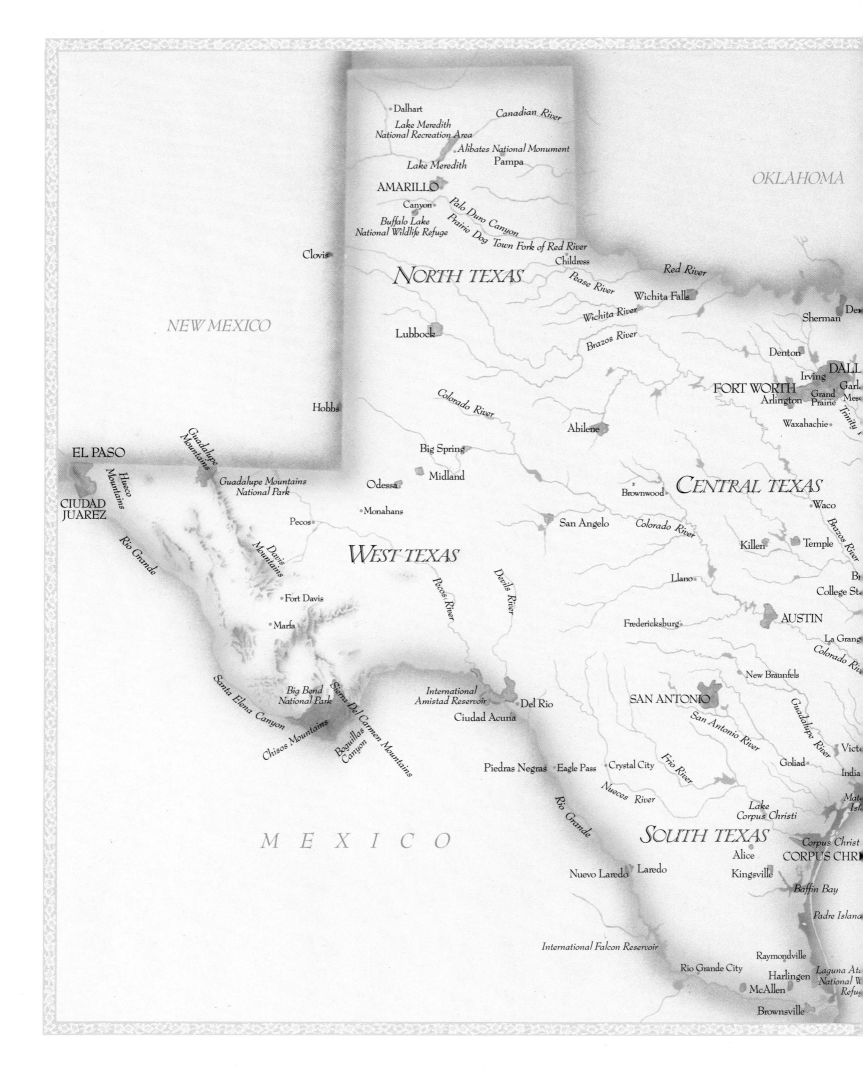

CONTENTS

A mass of bluebonnets, the state's favorite flower, blankets a hill in Central Texas.

PHOTO: STEPHAN MYERS

CENTRAL TEXAS

CENTRAL TEXAS
Prairies and hill country

⚜

*E*nchanted Rock creaks and hisses and moans, if you believe the legends. On moonlit nights, crystals glimmer and dance on the pink granite dome. Indians called the lights "spirit fires." An outcropping of pluton that cooled and solidified from earth's inner molten fuels a billion years ago, Enchanted Rock ascends a hundred yards and covers a square mile. It resembles a fair-skinned human knee, crooked in relaxation. Surrounded by blue hills and mesas, Enchanted Rock is about fifty miles southeast of the geographical center of Texas. And if this hillish country is the state's heartland, the granite dome speaks to its soul.

The vegetation reflects the state's range and diversity. Ferns crowd the shadows of boulders on the lower slopes. Crevices are compactly lined with delicate grasses and tiny scratch-daisies that bloom yellow in the fall. Only 1,825 feet above sea level, the summit is dimpled with bathtub-shaped depressions called vernal pools. Translucent fairy shrimp wriggle in the collected rainwater. As the water dissolves rock and evaporates, soil forms. Spikemoss and quillwort lead to thick stands of little bluestem and sideoats grama, the tufted and water-frugal midgrasses so characteristic of the Texas plains. Agarito, a sharp-leaved bush that produces sweet red berries, grows beside desert yucca and prickly pear. At the top of Enchanted Rock is a lone and thriving live oak. But the bluestem and grama dominate these unlikely and telling arboretums. The flora of Texas is best understood as *grassland striving to be*. Even in

*T*he flowers of skeleton plant are short-lived, opening only after the sun warms the air.

Scattered across rocky hills and pasturelands are plains prickly pear, the insect-pollinated yellow cups followed by bright red, edible fruits called "tunas."

Morning glory and Mexican hat

prairie climax, grasses need intermixed and balanced communities of legumes and forbs — plants that often brightly flower. In winter dormancy, the bluestem turns sorrel. Meanwhile, the wildflowers sprout green seedlings. And in spring, the burst of coreopsis turns these plant islands into orbs of flaming yellow dotted with maroon.

Indians stalked mammoths and giant bison here 12,000 years ago. Spaniards found the vicinity dominated first by Tonkawas, then by Apaches, and then by hated Comanches. Through cultural assimilation and regular theft of that revolutionary creature, the horse, the once-lowly Comanches made themselves the most powerful of the warlike nomads who followed the bison herds. Comanches named Enchanted Rock. Our science attributes the eerie sounds to the contraction and cooling of sun-heated rock. Indians, whose metaphysics of nature were not so detached and empirical, believed the place was sacred and haunted. Imagine the chills that must have traveled up the necks of Comanches who chased an Anglo-Texan surveyor up Enchanted Rock in 1841. Could they have known that this man, who holed up in the vernal pools and held them off with gunfire for three hours, was the Texans' most famous and brutal Indian fighter, Jack Hays? One legend features a white woman who escaped Indian captors and found refuge on Enchanted Rock. She went crazy, it was said, and the place still echoes her nightly screams.

A few miles north of Fredericksburg, Enchanted Rock is now a state park. Climbers stand crook-hipped and motionless, staring. Nowadays, the most reliable sound of Enchanted Rock comes from bawling cattle in pastures beyond the park. When ranchers first saw Texas, which was seventy percent prairie, they thought they could never deplete that pre-posterous grassland. But instead of occasional and beneficial harvest by migratory buffalo herds, the native prairie strains were subjected to constant grazing pressure by far too many cattle. Settlement and over-grazing extinguished the prairie fires that killed woody plants, allowing competing grasses to survive. Throughout Texas, the balance of grass-land has been reversed by the invasion of choking brush. So the hills around Enchanted Rock are blue with juniper, once prevalent only in rocky elevations and draws. Pastures fill up with sapling mesquites. The Texas Hill Country can look as wan and despoiled as the rocky terraces of ancient Greece, and this damage was done in little more than a century. Struggling ranchers now run goats as well as cattle. Goats eat brush.

And yet when spring comes, this land of harsh extremes, violent heritage, and thoughtless use, nurtures some of the most splendid color on earth. Forbs and legumes have fared better than the grasses. Once called buffalo clover—bison herds were thought to graze it—an

*O*ne plant of plains coreopsis isn't much to look
at. Put a million of them together and it's a show.
Spread acres of them beneath live oak trees on
boulder strewn slopes of the Hill Country
and it's spectacular.

endemic legume seeks slopes and tolerates poor soil, as long as it's well-drained. Spanish-speaking settlers named it *el conejo*, the rabbit, because its white-tipped lupine bloom reminded them of cottontails. Anglo-Texans named this plant the bluebonnet and institutionalized it as the state wildflower in 1901. Domestic cattle decline to graze it, which partly accounts for the solid blue slopes. Bluebonnets announce the spring; when March sends a late norther, the leguminous blooms sometimes poke up through the snow. In a few more weeks, yellow coreopsis fills the woodland meadows. Borrowing nourishment from the roots of grasses, the semiparasitic Indian paintbrush seeks moist ground and gathers on roadsides. As the days warm up, Engelmann evening primrose opens its white blossoms at sunset, welcoming the pollinating favors of night-flying moths.

Around Enchanted Rock, these acres of color are best enjoyed at a distance. A spring hike invites confrontation with western diamondback rattlesnakes. But the bitter comes balanced by the sweet. Flitting in the trees, as if to mirror the wildflowers, is a male painted bunting. It winters in the tropics and warbles like a vireo. Red and green and indigo—North America's most gaudily colored bird—this creature is so benign it finds itself bullied by cardinals.

Vines of leatherflower clamber over low brush and rocks, dangling showy pendants of lavender and purple. The flowers have no petals, but the thick sepals appear petallike and curl backwards, revealing the darker inner surface.

Opposite page:

Early spring moisture brings the tall clusters of creamy white bells of Buckley yucca to the Hill Country. Almost all parts of this plant were utilized by the Indian tribes that inhabited this region.

Counterposed terrain etches persistent lines through the state's interior. From the edge of pine forest that aligns East Texas with the nature and culture of the Old South, the tall-grass prairieland rolls westward to the abrupt slopes of rock hills, which delineate the midgrass plains and hint at deserts farther west. The names of Central Texas prairies define changing vegetative zones. The Fayette Prairie bridges the lower watersheds of the Colorado and Brazos rivers, the San Antonio Prairie angles northeast from the city of that name, the Grand Prairie crosses Red River into Oklahoma. The underlying soils can be waxy and black, sandy and red. But all these grasslands are part of the tall-grass prairie system that stunned pioneers from hot Texas to frigid Manitoba. The sea of switchgrass, Indiangrass, and big bluestem stood six feet tall, soughing in the breeze: Walt Whitman's leaves of grass.

The rock hills vary, too. Set off from the prairies and South Texas chaparral by the dramatic Balcones Escarpment, the Hill Country is most often associated with limestone outcroppings. But the Llano Uplift, which includes Enchanted Rock, features slabs and boulders of granite. Farther north, along the upper Brazos, the weathered bluffs are sandstone. These different hills form a modest *cordillera,* as Spanish-speaking settlers termed their mountain ranges, and from south to north the contrast of prairie and highlands holds true.

Climate corresponds. Although Texans traditionally place the limit of the thirty-inch rainfall at the 98th Meridian, it more correctly meanders along the line of hills. East of the rainfall barrier, the tall turf grasses can thrive and dominate; trees cluster in islands and winding groves that Anglo settlers called mottes. In the wooded hills to the west, bunchy midgrasses such as little bluestem and sideoats grama cope better with the unreliable moisture. These factors determined use and settlement. Members of Stephen F. Austin's colony thought the central prairies were an agricultural paradise. Once the Indians were conquered, the semiarid hills accommodated ranches and cowboys: the Old West.

Some natural historians believe that Texas's prime wildflower habitat was a moderately grazed Fayette Prairie. If so, it didn't last long. Farmers saw that ocean of grass and ventured logical projections: wheat, corn, rice, oats, sugar cane—domestic grasses all. They also plowed up the prairies for that Southern panacea, cotton. Still, they loved and valued the bounty of flowers. They dried and crushed a white-flowered composite, Philadelphia fleabane, and stuffed it in mattresses to repel fleas and bedbugs. They brewed its tea for sore throats and believed a fleabane poultice reduced swelling. Root tea from the nectar-rich butterfly weed was taken for heart trouble. One of Texas's loveliest blossoms, the bell-shaped scarlet clematis, grows on vines along shaded creek banks and river bottoms. Settlers prescribed its tea for migraine headaches.

*

Opposite page:

*W*isps of late evening sunlight touch a prairie phlox, highlighting the delicate blossom and the fuzziness of stem and leaf.

Following pages:

*E*arly morning sunlight sweeps across a field of Indian blanket, illuminating the red and gold of each flower.

*C*lumps of Texas prickly pear can become quite large, and when the spiny pads are rimmed with cups of apricot, they create a memorable spectacle.

Preferring plants and birds to people, a Scot named Thomas Drummond arrived on the central prairies in 1833—just in time for a cholera epidemic, a horrendous Brazos River flood known as the Great Overflow, and the angry ferment of the Texas Revolution. Though solitary outings were quite dangerous, the naturalist was always off in the woods and meadows, collecting specimens. The Drummond wild onion and Drummond phlox bear his name. Drummond's seeds made phlox the rage of European flowerbeds. He collected more than seven hundred species of plants, but the cholera killed him.

Later, German immigrants made an extraordinary contribution to Texas botany. One group arrived at the port of Indianola in 1845 and found that all the mule teamsters had gone south to profit from the U.S. war with Mexico. The Germans had to walk to Balcones Escarpment, and dozens of them died along the way. Trying to keep their spirits up, they danced at night to a clarinet played by an overworked gravedigger.

The Hill Country Germans established New Braunfels at the foot of limestone cliffs. The lush townsite was watered by the cypress-lined Guadalupe River and an emerald, spring-fed tributary that raised fogs of steam in the winter. A Protestant minister, Louis Ervendberg, collected grasses and corresponded with the famous English botanist, Asa Gray. Ferdinand Lindheimer, editor of the *Zeitung* newspaper, collected plants with such energy and expertise that twenty species are named for him —among them Lindheimer muhly grass and the wildflowers Lindheimer beebalm, Lindheimer senna, Lindheimer tephrosia, and Texas yellow star. Around the offshoot settlement of Fredericksburg, Germans planted peach trees, dragged up rocks to build their fences, and considered how much easier life would be if they could get along with Comanches. Ferdinand von Roemer, a geologist and wildflower enthusiast for whom the two-leaved senna is named, observed the Indian-camp negotiation of the white settlers' only enduring peace treaty with the Comanches. From New Braunfels, von Roemer then rode a stage to Galveston to catch a boat home to Germany. Collecting along the way, he rhapsodized about a prairie awash with bluebonnets, milkworts, beard-tongue, evening primrose, and morning glories.

Other enthusiasts simply responded to the aesthetics. Generations of Texas women have identified wildflowers as a hobby and painted them with a passion. Eliza Johnston was married to Albert Sidney Johnston, who as a Confederate general died at Shiloh. But in the 1850s he was a U.S. Army major ordered to Texas's Indian frontier. A line of forts along the *cordillera* protected prairie settlers from Indian raids. Johnston served the forts as paymaster, and his wife often traveled with him. She painted rain lilies, mesquite beans, and the tunas of prickly pear. Even the caustic

*T*he abundant pollen and nectar of Indian blanket attracts numerous insects, especially butterflies, bees, and beetles.

A small crab spider waits patiently to dine on some tiny insect that might visit the pollen-rich stamens of white prickly poppy.

Opposite page:
*S*neezeweed follows moisture-retaining stream banks, fills rock crevices, and grows around the edges of boulders, making splashes of eye-catching gold.

bull nettle, she noted, is graced by a fragrant, jasminelike blossom. Calling Indian blanket by its other name, the firewheel, Eliza Johnston illustrated the dark red, yellow-tipped gaillardia with a pollinating moth veiled in camouflage. She composed her caption:

Of this flower is related a very pretty tradition by the Mexicans—the flower was originally of bright golden hue, and the favourite of the unfortunate Aztec. The young maidens delighted in decorating their jetty hair with a diadem of its golden discs, and the lithe limbs of the little children were caressed by its sunny petals as they sported on the glorious Prairies of their happy land; but it was the will of the Almighty that this should not last. Cortez came! and the lovely land was deluged with the blood of its innocent and confiding inhabitants; the loved flower in pity caught the sanguinary stream as it fell, and to this day has remained stained a deep red, and now when the tiny butterfly of its own colour is seen flitting around it, they say, ''Tis the spirit of the Aztec watching in gratitude his favourite flower.'

The culture of the buffalo Indians would not last another half-century. We know that Comanches chewed mesquite leaves for acid indigestion and gargled a root tea of purple coneflowers for sore throats. They sniffed

purple sneezeweed to force spasms in childbirth, boiled thistle roots for gonorrhea, treated eye irritations with the sap of prickly poppies, and believed nightshade tonic was good for tuberculosis. A sense of their aesthetics is harder to come by. Comanches left no written language, and oral historians thought of them too late. The most poignant tale of those savage years offers one clue. Stolen at age nine when Comanches raided a Brazos prairie settlement in 1836, Cynthia Ann Parker lived among them on the plains until 1860. She married a famous warrior, and one of her sons, Quanah Parker, was the Comanches' last free war chief. In a raid on a Pease River camp, Texas rangers ran her down as a fleeing hostile. Along with her infant daughter, she was returned to the grassland farmers. By every token but blood, Cynthia Ann Parker was a Comanche. When her daughter died at age five, she mutilated herself in grief and starved herself to death. The child's name was Prairie Flower.

⚘

Whether forming low mounds in prairies and pastures or cascading down a rocky slope, Dakota vervain has finely cut foliage that adds a lacy background to purple clusters.

Immigrant farmers from Central Europe often spared a few acres as they found them. Aside from these relict patches, scattered roadsides, old cemeteries, and a few large tracts along the Red River that are harvested as hay meadows, Texas's share of the tall-grass prairie no longer exists. Prairies can come back from overgrazing, but once the plow breaks the soil, virgin grassland is gone forever. On the ranches, many stockmen have planted range grasses native to India, South Africa, and the Eurasian steppes. In the sandstone hills, the Brazos has been tamed by a flood-control reservoir with a charming name, Possum Kingdom. The vegetative boundary associated with the Balcones Escarpment and the 98th Meridian has gained another line of demarcation—the multilane highway called Interstate 35. But the weather hasn't changed much, and neither has the color. As if to mollify their sufferers, a hot dry summer followed by a cold wet winter guarantees a bumper crop of Texas wildflowers.

John R. Thomas, a bald and muscular man in his early forties, reflected on that floral paradox in late 1986. "Take bluebonnets," he said. "When the blooms die, a thick mat of seeds is left on the ground. If those seeds get a lot of rain in the summer, they continue to germinate. The summer sprouts die before they can bloom again, and that depletes the supply of seeds for the next spring. A little drought conserves them. And a hard winter helps bluebonnets, especially if there's a lot of frozen precipitation, because that sets back competing grasses."

John Thomas grew up on a ranch and rice farm near Eagle Lake, between Houston and San Antonio. He studied business, not botany, in college, and his approach to wildflowers was that of a farmer. When the agricultural economy soured in the early seventies, he looked for a steadier income in the cities. Amused that developers tried to cover large

*B*efore the plow and the bulldozer disturbed the
land, dense stands of bluebonnets like this one
covered much of the state.

In a small crevice at Enchanted Rock, thelesperma finds sufficient moisture to open flat yellow flowers atop slender, wiry stems.

The flat, conspicuously netted and veined petals of green-flowered milkvine offer a convenient landing platform for passing insects.

Opposite page:
The lovely flowers of stiff-stem flax must be appreciated in the field, for it drops its petals only moments after being picked.

tracts of cleared land with the same expensive squares of turf they rooted on their suburban lawns, he pitched the rustic idea that grasses grow more affordably from planted seeds; as a rancher and grassman, he could even supply the equipment. In 1983, a Houston client asked the revegetating contractor if he could do the same thing with wildflowers.

Joining the movement, Thomas found a dearth of bulk seeds but a wealth of patron saints. Foremost among them was Lady Bird Johnson. As First Lady, she championed wildflowers as the best resource of Texas's parks and roadsides, and her influence and power no doubt generated new enthusiasm and research funding within the state's universities. After her husband left the Presidency and they returned to the Johnson City ranch, she facilitated the complex and expensive negotiations that made nearby Enchanted Rock—which was in eventual danger of ranchette real estate development—into the state park that saved it. In that case, she worked both with politicians and the Nature Conservancy, a private organization with national headquarters in Washington and a Texas office in San Antonio. Raising money from corporations, foundations, and affluent individuals, the group purchases valued and endangered nature sites and then negotiates with governmental officials to make the tracts state or national parks. In retirement, Mrs. Johnson donated land and founded a National Wildflower Research Center on the outskirts of Austin. And yet the grounds of the presidential ranch house at Johnson City had never blossomed to her satisfaction. John Thomas's company, Wildseed, Inc., planted the mix that made her front yard bloom.

In a small plane, Thomas searches the rolling land around Bellville, Brenham, and Bryan for bluebonnet stands that, from the air, look like small lakes. His young native plants specialist, Ray Ullrich, spends the spring driving Central Texas farm roads, chatting on front porches with old-timers, offering them leases for a cash crop they never imagined they had. Ullrich maps the bluebonnet's best range as a rough diamond bounded by Corpus Christi, Victoria, Huntsville, Waxahachie, Brownwood, Brady, and Fredericksburg. Between the *cordillera* and a line due north from Brownsville, the blooms of Texas paintbrush compose a pink corridor, 150 miles wide, from the Rio Grande Valley to Oklahoma. Looking for stands of Mexican hat, Ullrich follows the Colorado River. Thomas said they don't have to leave Eagle Lake to find the coreopsis. "If you plow up an old rice field that's been farmed to death, soaked with herbicides, and do nothing more at all, in the spring it comes up solid coreopsis. It just floats with yellow."

They contract with growers in Germany and Holland for wine-cup and meadow-pink seeds. To supplement their Texas leases, they plant row crops of wildflowers at Eagle Lake. They harvest the elusive seeds with modified farm equipment. Some are gathered by a rotating bristle brush, others by a contraption that looks like a tractor fitted with an eight-snorkeled vacuum cleaner. To the delight and challenge of a hometown metalworker, the planting equipment must accommodate the weight, hardness, spacing needs, and germinating depth of different seeds, all sown together. With mixes that run from bluebonnets to gayfeathers to horsemint, the contractors try to allow for variables of weather and soil: in one season, some color will cover it all.

Commingling desert, mountain, plains, and even tropical vegetation, about 2,500 wildflower species appear in Texas. The size of the state accounts for that. As large geopolitical entities of temperate latitude go, the range and variety of flora is not phenomenal. Profusion makes Texas a special wildflower habitat: whole canvases of color, not the single brush strokes. "Our stiffest competition is nature," said John Thomas. "People say, 'Can you give us what we see from the highway at fifty-five miles an hour? We want two hundred acres of yellow. Two hundred acres of blue.'"

Opposite page:
The numerous brown and yellow flowers of Mexican hat resemble sombreros and can be seen along roadsides and on rocky slopes of even the driest plains.

*Wedged between granite boulders, lace cactus
finds a bit of soil and, with spring rains, puts forth
flowers so large they dwarf the wickedly
spined base.*

*P*etals of the lace cactus surround
numerous stamens loaded with pollen that
awaits insect visitors.

*W*hile not a native wildflower, the corn poppy is occasionally planted in yards and along roadsides, where it mingles beautifully with the native white prickly poppy.

PHOTO: PAUL M. MONTGOMERY

*S*weet-scented, nectar-filled blossoms of phacelia
attract numerous species of butterflies, especially
the skippers.

Left:

*I*n cool, clear-flowing streams, water-willow forms
large colonies, the dark green foliage making a
lovely background for the unusual white flowers
streaked and blotched with purple.

*S*weet nectar deep within the blossoms of Dakota
vervain attracts many insects — in this case the
female to the food, the male to the female.

Right:
*F*ragile petals of erect dayflower shimmer in early
morning light but will soon be closed by the heat
of midday.

Plains black-foot prefers the dry soils of deserts, rocky hills, and slopes to flaunt its snow-white flowers.

Right:
Once an important food, medicine, and dye plant of indigenous Americans, the wild species of the weak-stemmed sunflower is now mostly left to the enjoyment of various insects, birds, and other small creatures.

Given half a chance, desert lantana will form large colonies in pastures and along roadside fences. Its toughness and multitude of lovely flowers have made it a favorite for cultivation. Its nectar is much appreciated by numerous insect species, especially bees and butterflies.

Left:

Clambering over low shrubbery and fences or sprawling on the ground in heaps, sharp-pod morning glory opens large trumpets of deep lavender in the early morning coolness. Hummingbirds, bees, and butterflies all partake of the plentiful nectar hidden deep in the throat of the widely expanding flower.

*The delicate fragrance and intense whiteness of
the evening-opening flowers of gaura attract
numerous moths, their primary pollinators. As the
flowers begin to fade the next morning, they become
a deep pink or rosy red.*

Right:
*After each warm-weather rain, the fragrant
blossoms of Drummond rain lily appear overnight,
often covering large areas with intoxicating
loveliness.*

A perfect, many-layered arrangement of sepals conceals the budding fluffy lavender flowers of nodding thistle.

Right:
A native of Europe, nodding thistle has spread rapidly westward, covering the rangeland with large, prickly flowers.

*W*ith flowers among the most intricately shaped
in the world, passionflower vines sprawl or
climb over low shrubbery and fences, flaunting the
exotic blossoms throughout the season.

Left:
*O*ne of our common wildflowers, pink evening
primrose forms spectacular ribbons of white, pink or
rose along most roadsides in spring and
early summer.

*T*ropical in its vividness and uniquely shaped
flowers, butterfly weed graces fields, pastures, and
roadside fencerows with large clusters of brilliant
red-orange. It is a favorite with butterflies, which
seek nourishment from the nectar-filled cups of
each fragrant blossom.

*I*n areas of almost solid rock, yellow stonecrop
sinks tenacious roots deep into the narrowest
cracks and crevices and in early spring spreads
tiny, succulent leaves and bright yellow flowers
across the barren surface.

In the first warming days of spring, blue-eyed
grass opens tiny flowers of deepest azure. Normally
growing in low clumps but covering large areas, the
flowers form almost solid sheets of blue.

Right:

*B*earing blossoms like small, exquisite orchids,
crameria nestles among low-lying grasses, hidden
from all except the most observant eyes.

*In June, Texas thistle brightens unmowed
meadows and pastures, the pincushionlike flowers
a mecca for bees, beetles, and butterflies alike.*

Left:
*Deep-throated blossoms of ivory and old rose are
almost hidden by the large leaves of devil's-claw.
The unflattering common name describes the
seedpod, which splits into two, sharp-pointed,
curved spines at maturity.*

The black stigma of day-primrose is quite showy against the crinkly, crepe-paper-textured petals. It differs from its close relative, the evening primrose, by remaining open during the entire day.

*I*nsects, such as these brightly colored soldier
beetles, are lured to the greenish blossoms of
antelope-horns by a heady fragrance and a rich
feast of nectar and pollen.

Following pages:
*R*ippling across rocky hills and slopes,
thelesperma greets early spring in undulating
sheets of gold.

*Herbage of this plant is very bitter to the taste,
hence the common name of bitterweed. But the
pretty flowers blend with other springtime favorites
to make roadsides gay with color.*

Left:

*A persistent nuisance it sometimes may be, but
when viewed along a roadside or a meadow's edge,
the Texas dandelion has a special beauty
all its own.*

*T*railing slender stems along the ground or
sprawling over low-growing grasses, wine-cup holds
its satiny, magenta-colored petals upright,
surrounding a central column of
pollen-laden stamens.

Right:

*O*n almost shrublike growth, poppy-mallow
raises wine-colored cups skyward, catching the
early rays of a spring morning.

EAST TEXAS

EAST TEXAS

Timberlands

⚜

Signaled perhaps by the even measure of darkness and light, monarch butterflies fly north each year precisely on the spring equinox. In mountainous central Mexico, where the monarchs winter in about twenty forest groves, people hear a soft fluttering whisper from the millions of orange and black wings. Spanning up to five generations, the annual migration will take them as far as Canada and Maine. Glider pilots have encountered monarchs at 10,000 feet. The butterflies mate in their migratory flight, and by the time they drift in twos and threes through the shadowed woods of East Texas, the females bulge with eggs. They always lay them on milkweed, their only food supply.

In sandy meadows and sunny borders along the pines, the monarchs search for milkweeds. Humans have invested milkweeds with a wide range of purgative and stimulant medicinal qualities; they make ropes from its stem fibers and glue from its milky sap. Monarch butterflies base an entire system of life support on sugary compounds in the milkweed. Along with nutrients, these glycocides impart a cardiac poison that nauseates birds and mice. The absorbed chemical toxicity survives the monarch's passage from egg to caterpillar to chrysalis. Though some predators have adapted, learning to eat bodily parts with lesser concentrations of the poison, most leave the butterflies alone.

In openings of the upland woods, bees wriggle face down, insistently, in crimson clover. The petals of the small blooms are elongated and

S*pider lily, a denizen of semishaded swamps.*

Previous pages: T*he pageantry of coreopsis and Indian paintbrush.*

*F*lowering in the cool of spring, crimson clover cloaks pastures and roadsides in dark red velvet. A protein-rich legume, it is an important forage crop for livestock and wild game.

pointed in the same direction, which prevents most insects from reaching the nectar and pollen. As the bees probe the flowers for food, they rub against the pistils and stamens of different plants, collecting and transferring the pollen dust. Pollinated almost exclusively by bees, crimson clover is an exotic in Texas. Native to Europe, it was first grown as a field crop by Spaniards in the Netherlands, when they ruled Holland. Crimson clover is a valuable plant. The legume root system releases nitrogen in the soil. Cattle and deer graze the protein-rich foliage in grass-poor winter. Flowering in the cool spring, it cloaks pastures in dark red velvet.

But among botanists and naturalists, the term exotic has a pejorative taint. Introduced species often run amok in new environments. They crowd out native species and become pest weeds. In northeast Texas, state highway crews and private organizations have sown crimson clover for roadside beautification. Critics maintain that the clover's dense and aggressive foliage stifles native wildflower competitors, leaving only roadside grasses nine months out of the year. But in spring, the blooming clover draws narrowing, parallel lines of scarlet between the highway shoulders and trees. On the divided interstates, it transforms dull medians into ornamental hummocks: red carpets of travel, in soothing effect.

To the critics' eyes, the rural boulevards of crimson clover look forced and voracious in this part of the state. Native wildflowers of East Texas fill the spaces between the trees. They lurk in small dimensions in the shade. Here their colors paint corridors and patches, not vistas. Juxtaposed against the rest of the state, the timberlands have the look and feel of another country. Rain and soil set the forest region dramatically apart.

⚜

In far West Texas, near El Paso, the desert gets by on eight inches of rainfall a year; eastward over the plains and Edwards Plateau, the precipitation gradually increases to thirty inches. The forty-inch line runs north from Matagorda Bay, intersects an oak and hickory forest bearded with Spanish moss, and, near Oklahoma, cuts through a finger of the blackland prairie. Farther east are the piney woods which on maps resemble a knife blade cutting in from the Louisiana border. At the knife point, near Texarkana, annual rainfall averages forty-eight inches. At the hilt, near Beaumont, the state's soggiest residents expect fifty-six inches.

Upthrusting mountain ranges and heavy ocean sediment tilted the foundation of East Texas away from an Eocene sea. This ancient sea washed back and forth with the spread and thaw of the polar ice caps, depositing layers of sediment. During the melts, churning rivers laid silt. From these origins, sandy and loam soils now prevail, but clay soils are also scattered through the region, and often the loose sands rest on beds

Opposite page:

*L*ong, conspicuously curled stamens characterize the dainty flowers of blue-curls, which thrive in the dappled shade of woodland edges and openings.

of the compacted clay. Grains of sand are the largest kind of soil particles. For plants, the composition of sand provides excellent aeration and drainage, but the retention of moisture and nutrients is poor. Though the region of East Texas was grassland ten million years ago, trees dominate its appearance now. The variety of forest species approaches that of the state's wildflowers. During the Ice Ages, the northern forest retreated from the glaciers and left American beech and mockernut hickory in the company of southerners like magnolia and longleaf pine.

Under the deciduous hardwoods, most wildflowers bloom early, before the overstory of spring leaves blocks out the sun. Evergreens present a more hostile environment. Along with the constant shade of the forest floor, the mat of rotting pine needles mulches out competing seedlings and acidifies the rainwater. The acidity leaches calcium from the soil and makes it even more infertile. Still, trees and shrubs belong to the class of angiosperms, or flowering plants. To find the best color in East Texas, sometimes it helps to look up. Especially in the sandy uplands that curve northeastward from the Nacogdoches Escarpment, flowering dogwoods bathe the spring woods in frothy cream. Dogwoods also contribute one of the handsomest reds of the autumn leaves. No less striking is a thorny shrub called the coral bean. Blooming from a spike

A young seedling of longleaf pine puts forth its silvery "candle" in early spring.

Tiny fungi feed on the decomposing leaf litter covering the forest floor.

Opposite page:
In the East Texas timberlands, most wildflowers bloom early, before the deciduous hardwoods leaf out, blocking the sun.

The striking bloom spikes of the coral bean emerge from the roots, not the leaves, of the shrubby plant. The flowers mature into drooping black pods which crack open and offer brilliantly colored, deadly poisonous seeds.

A familiar sight on the lakes and ponds in East Texas, turtles line up on a protruding log to bask in the early spring sun.

Opposite page:
Tolerant of a range of habitats, bald cypress trees that grow in standing water raise "knees" that allow their root systems to breathe.

that emerges from the roots, not the leaves, the branched red flower produces a drooping black legume. In turn, the pod cracks and offers an array of brilliantly colored, deadly poisonous seeds. With this plant, Indians placed a higher premium on aesthetics than practicality. Coral beans were exchanged as items of trade.

Covered with oak and pine, the rolling sand hills reach an altitude of 500 feet. The other face of East Texas is low and swampy, given to tupelo and cypress. Flood patterns can change these forests quickly. On early nineteenth century maps, a large area of northeast Texas was written off as an uninhabitable obstacle called the Great Swamp. East of present Texarkana, the Red River bends in Arkansas and angles southward through Louisiana, becoming a much larger stream as it approaches the mouth of the Mississippi River. Around A.D. 1200, according to one theory, the backwash from a huge Mississippi flood initiated the Red River logjam called the Great Raft. Carried by the Red's annual freshets, durable cypress and cedar trees accumulated faster at one end than they rotted at the other. By the 1830s, the continuous log dams were strung out for 165 miles in Louisiana, which wreaked havoc with the ecology of northeast Texas.

The obstructed river deposited silt and spread laterally into lakes, bayous, and sloughs. The Great Raft probably created Caddo Lake, though popular legend attributes that body of water to a prehistoric earthquake. The outflow deepened Cypress Creek enough for steamboats to navigate as far inland as Jefferson and load cargoes of baled cotton. Humans

Left:
The timberlands of East Texas are an extension of America's southern mixed forest. In Caddo Lake State Park, indigenous hardwoods rise to primeval heights.

A mayfly is trapped in a spider's web.

attacked the Great Raft first with sturdy boats employed as battering rams, then with nitroglycerine, then with channel dredging. When the Red flowed freely for the first time in centuries, tributary creeks and bayous began to run faster, digging deeper channels. Drained swamps turned into grassland. The imagined riverport of Jefferson languished as a quaint backwoods town. As the soil compositions, drainage patterns, and forest species change, so do the wildflowers, though the transition can take eons. Southern iris and water-primrose, which grow in mud, eventually yield to purple pleat-leaf and purple coneflower, which favor sandy prairie.

Human settlement transformed East Texas in many ways, and much faster. Loggers began to thin the region's trees for use as furniture and lumber, even baseball bats. To large timber companies, slow-growing hickory and oak trees were pest growth. Clear-cutting replaced the hardwoods with plantations of fast-growing pines. Clear-cutting drove the magnificent ivory-billed woodpecker into probable extinction, and pine farms hardly enhanced the growth of wildflowers. Ecologists consider them biological deserts. But nature foiled planters who cleared the trees for cotton and grain. After a few harvests, the acidic and easily depleted soil left fields fallow, farmhouses empty and falling down. The timberlands are filled now with abandoned fields, and these often become wildflower meadows: brown-eyed susan, partridge pea, downy goldenrod, standing cypress, spring beauty, passionflower, blazing star. Sprawling colonies of pointed phlox bloom in association with sandwort, blue-eyed grass, yellow star-grass, and Indian paintbrush. The pert white cups of sandwort nicely counterpose the subtle sandyland bluebonnets. The latter plants' common names emphasize their soil requirements.

Of the frontier naturalists, a shy, Connecticut-born Yale graduate named Charles Wright was the East Texas pioneer. On the advice of a Yale president who had no first-hand knowledge of life and academics in wilderness outposts, at twenty-five Wright accepted a tutorial position in Natchez, Mississippi, in 1836. Glad to quit that community of gamblers, prostitutes, and outlaws, Wright entered the Republic of Texas and remained fifteen years, through early statehood and the Mexican War. Working as a surveyor and schoolteacher, he developed a lifelong friendship with Asa Gray, the Cambridge and Harvard botanist. Gray later arranged for Wright to accompany a military boundary commission through the regions of El Paso, New Mexico, and Arizona; subsequent expeditions found Wright collecting in South Africa, Japan, Cuba, and Nicaragua.

In southeast Texas, between the Neches and Sabine rivers, for seven years he studied plants and hunted deer, making their skins into leggings

Though not a native, Japanese honeysuckle is now firmly entrenched in the Texas flora. The tough, rampantly spreading vines are often a nuisance but do produce appealing masses of fragrant flowers in early spring.

Opposite page:

Among spring's earliest delights are the violets, which open large, sweet-scented flowers in abundance along roadsides and in damp, open woodlands.

*A frog breaks the still surface
of a quiet woodland lake,
surveying his domain for food
or an enemy.*

and moccasins. Among the wildflowers named for Wright was the yellow Simpson rosinweed (*Silphium simpsonii* var. *Wrightii*)—Indians and settlers' children used its resinous sap for chewing gum. But the Sabine country was filled with murderers and thieves. Surveyors of scholarly bent had to contend with land hustlers who dealt in counterfeit deeds. The Indian-baiting policies of Mirabeau Lamar had stirred the local tribes' hostility. By 1844, when Wright joined the faculty of Texas's first college at Rutersville, near LaGrange, he was eager to see the last of those swamps and trees.

For people who perceive of Texas as a land of spare features and astounding sky, the forest region can be a dark, brooding, and forbidding place. The spookiness is partly claustrophobic, but not altogether fanciful. In nature and culture, the Texas timberlands are an extension of America's southern mixed forest—a reminder of Smoky and Blue Ridge mountain ranges, the bayous of Cajun Louisiana. From the mouth of the Sabine to Anahuac, even the coastline derives its character from the Deep South. Silt flushed into the Gulf by the Mississippi River fans out and washes back ashore, creating a geologically young system of chenier beaches, chenier marches, chenier ridges, and chenier plains. The word comes from the French *chene*, or oak, the dominant forest species. Contemporary songwriters evoke the region's natural charm. Sweet magnolia, tupelo honey. Sap running from the sweet gum trees carries a fine scent of fall.

⚜

The Big Thicket once covered more than three million acres of the wettest part of the state. Inland from Beaumont, northward through the Trinity, Neches, and Sabine river drainage systems, the woods receive up to sixty inches of rain a year. One hundred and ten days of the year, the temperature exceeds ninety degrees. It reaches freezing only twenty days of the year. A close relative of tropical rain forests, the thicket has their dark mood and primal flavor.

The resident Indians were Alabamas, Coushattas, and Cherokees. During the Civil War, white men known as jayhawkers vanished in the woods to dodge the rebel draft. Their wives and children left food and clothing for them in the crooks and hollows of trees. In Hardin County, near Union Wells and Bad Luck creeks, a hundred-acre tract called Kaiser's Burnout commemorates a Confederate officer who set fire to one refuge of jayhawkers. For eighty years the forest showed evidence of Captain Kaiser's wrath. Some jayhawkers were conscientious objectors and Union sympathizers. They admired Sam Houston, who had opposed Secession. Others were simply poor whites, and they did not wish to lose their lives in a war fought over the rich planters' labor pool of black slaves.

*In May and June sweet bay is starred with flowers
of incredible fragrance and creamy color
and texture.*

Forming large clumps in pastures or trailing over fences and low shrubbery, wild pink rose opens clusters of delicate fragrant pink flowers from spring through latest summer.

Grass-pink, a native orchid, is found in the fragile habitat where savannahs grade into the slightly lower and wetter acid bogs.

The Big Thicket's settlers hunted game in the river and creek bottoms and introduced the region's most formidable exotics, razorback hogs. They slashed the pigs' ears to brand them and turned them loose to fatten on acorns and beech and hickory nuts. They rounded up the hogs periodically with fierce howling dogs. After a few generations of reversion to the wild, the hogs exhibit once again the razor-sharp tusks of their boarish ancestors. With a sound like pistol shots, the feral hogs pop these tusks when they're hounded and angry.

The region's last red wolves roam in Jefferson County and across the Louisiana border, but they're outnumbered now by cousins interbred with coyotes and dogs. Eight-foot alligators whack their tails and glide in chocolate-colored water. In backwoods' stills, human occupants make clear whiskey that tastes like fair tequila but feels like swallowed gasoline, the next morning. On a disused logging road near the village of Saratoga, a mysterious light glimmers in the woods at night. Swamp gas, maybe. According to the legend, a hunter fell asleep on a railroad spur and was decapitated by a train. The elusive Ghost Light is said to be his lantern, swaying as he searches for his head.

Fires that helped maintain vegetative balance are fought now by humans with lives and property at stake. The biological crossroads of the Big Thicket have been devastated by loggers' clear-cutting. Ivory-billed woodpeckers were last seen here. Oil drilling and production flush ruinous salt water into the swamps and bayous, a contamination fought by rice farmers along the southern clearings. Almost too late, in the 1970s conservationists and Texas Senator Ralph Yarborough persuaded the federal government to create a Big Thicket Preserve of 84,500 acres; nine representative forest units and three stream corridors are scattered in six southeast Texas counties. Still, even in an altered and diminished habitat, the variety of flowers in the Big Thicket matches its wild contrast of terrain.

Interspersed with bluebells and herbertia, mixed tall-grass prairie covers the dark clay and sandy loam soils along the western edge. On sandy, calcium-leached hills in the northern thicket, bluestem grass and longleaf pine predominate; bird's-foot violet, wine-cup, and rose vervain flourish in the partial shade. Sandy soils underlaid by impermeable cemented hardpan, foster a slightly wetter grassland, with stunted black gum trees joining the longleaf pines. Adjusting to the elevation and fluctuating water tables of these savannahs are grass-pinks, meadow beauties, rose-mallows, yellow fringed orchids, and the delicate whorls of snowy orchids. On upland slopes, Carolina lilies freckle the floor of towering beech and loblolly pine forests, fragrant in summer with wafts of blooming magnolia. Near the Louisiana border in Newton County is

A solitary blossom of red buckeye lifts high its pollen-covered stamens, an enticing invitation for passing insects.

"In the baygalls, the larger and more biologically diverse swamps, fragrant water lilies bloom amid their pads of floating leaves."

Opposite page:
The intriguing flowers of the spider lily open from plants deeply rooted in the mud of backwater sloughs and marshes.

a lush and extravagantly perfumed spot called Wild Azalea Canyon.

And yet for all the rain, parts of the thicket look like semidesert. Louisiana yucca and eastern prickly pear occupy dry and rather barren ground amid oaks and farkleberry shrubs. Deep pockets of infertile white sand, which fail to hold the rainwater and reflect intense heat and glare from the sun, account for the thicket's most surprising vegetation. The rare trailing phlox, an endemic plant of this contradictory habitat, blooms only in the Big Thicket.

Elsewhere in the forest, dark water scarcely moves. Rotting leaves stain the bayous with tannic acid. Oaks and palmettos form dense jungles on poorly drained flats of clay, the flood plains of extinct rivers. In the fertile bottoms of rivers and creeks that regularly overflow, oaks and sweet gums achieve enormous size. With a resourcefulness often found in tropical jungles, woody cross-vines climb by leafy tendrils, seeking rays of sun for their handsome flowers. Taking a scientific name from Greek words that suggest beauty and sex, spider lilies bloom in the mud. Characteristic of inundated sloughs, bald cypress trees, in the company of water tupelos, raise "knees" that let their root systems breathe. Rooted in decaying stumps and logs, nodding-nixies bloom in the fall. Ferns stand shoulder-high.

Hydrogen sulfide bubbles from the submerged and rotting mat of foliage in the acid bogs. Water-spider orchids bloom on floating mats of sphagnum moss. Baygalls, the larger and more biologically diverse swamps, take their name from prevalent sweet bay trees and gallberry

holly shrubs. Fragrant water lilies bloom amid their pads of floating leaves. Though the dark, clear water rarely exceeds wading depth, some baygalls are a mile across. Jack Gore Baygall is an eerie, directionless place. People get lost in there. Indians bestowed the swamp with strong spirits, not all of them benevolent. It was a refuge of jayhawkers.

Wildflowers make their own concessions to this strange environment. Of the five carnivorous plants found in the United States, four are natives of the Big Thicket. They devour animal matter because the habitat does not fully meet their needs. Suspended in acid bogs and baygalls on star-shaped air sacs, the branches of floating bladderwort trap small marine organisms and hold them underwater until they decompose. In the longleaf and black gum savannahs, small butterworts mire insects on greasy and fleshy leaves that slowly enfold the prey. With tiny pink or rose-colored flowers, annual sundew seizes ants and other invertebrates with clear reddish glue exuded by gland-tipped hairs on the leaves.

Standing up like green-hooded cobras, pitcher plants are the thicket's showiest insectivores. They produce single, gracefully drooping, greenish yellow flowers. Veined with red, the leaves form a cylinder which collects rainwater, hence the plant's name. Insects that fall into these botanical cisterns cannot climb out. Moths and small grasshoppers rot in the collected water, imparting nutrients the pitcher plant fails to get from the nitrogen-poor soil. Nature usually gives as much as it takes. A few days after a fire, new pitcher plants shoot from the soil. In time, flies spiral neatly down the foliage wells and lay eggs on the decaying insect mass. Hatched by the warmth, the larvae eat their way out.

PHOTO: DOUG WILLIAMS

Lifting curved sprays of long-based red and yellow stars above the duff of a woodland forest, Indian pink greets the spring.

Opposite page:

Gland-tipped hairs on the leaves of annual sundew exude a sticky fluid that entraps ants and other tiny insects that the plant uses as food.

Texas wildflowers

*M*eadow pinks are among the most engaging of
wildflowers. Always seen in colonies, they splash
the roadsides and meadows with color and are
equally at home in the cultivated flower garden,
where they readily self-sow.

Left:
*T*uber vervain forms long, undulating ribbons of
color along open, sunny roadsides — an open feast
for numerous species of butterflies.

PHOTO: GEYATA AJILVSGI

From early March into June, primrose-leaved violet produces fragrant clouds of white in moist meadows, open woods and along stream banks.

Right:
"On upland slopes, Carolina lilies freckle the floor of towering beech and loblolly pine forests . . ."

An uncommon shrub, mock orange can occasionally be found along shaded stream banks in the East Texas woodlands. In late spring it dangles fragrant snow-white flowers in one-sided terminal clusters.

*One of the most common springtime wildflowers,
Indian paintbrush is nonetheless among the
showiest and most brightly colored. Large, leaflike
bracts surrounding the insignificant yellow flowers
give this plant its color.*

During warm summer days, pastures and woodlands are adorned with the shimmering beauty of wild pink rose.

Left:
Opening clusters of fuchsia pink before the leaves put forth, redbud trees froth the woodlands with early spring color.

White-topped umbrella grass is not a grass but a
sedge. The plant is named for the decorative, green-
tipped white bracts surrounding its terminal cluster
of tiny white flowers.

*W*hen a catalpa tree blooms, every branch is
tipped with a cluster of fragrant, orchidlike flowers.

*Bulbs of wild onion are both edible and delicious
— the clusters of fragrant pink and white flowers
providing a beautiful bonus.*

Right:

*Basket flower, a common native of uncommon
beauty, grows almost throughout the state.*

By early summer brown-eyed Susan is growing profusely along almost every roadside, the brown and golden-yellow blossoms making massed bouquets.

Right:

Often opening before the last snow, if given a warm, sunny day, spring beauty will form its own "snow," flaunting thousands of pink-striped white blossoms and covering large areas in lawns, fields and pastures.

*Entirely lacking in chlorophyll, Indian pipe
derives all its nourishment from decayed vegetable
matter in the soil. The plants have a succulent,
waxlike appearance and are usually snow-white
except for an occasional pink or rose specimen.*

Right:
*White dog's-tooth violet hangs wide-spreading
bells across wooded, gently rolling slopes in early
spring. It takes as long as seven years to produce a
flowering plant from seed.*

Resembling a burst of fire in the night sky, the flower of longleaf milkweed emits a fragrance reminiscent of tuberose and honeysuckle. The perfume can be quite heavy when the flowers bloom en masse along roadsides and woodland edges.

Right:
In deep, sandy soils flame-flower raises small, delicate petals on threadlike stems above succulent foliage.

In spring the greenish, tube-shaped flowers of
great Solomon's seal are strung in pairs beneath
the leaves, followed in summer by blue-
black berries.

*R*esembling a small rose, to which family it belongs, a sulphur cinquefoil blossom offers a fragrant, open face of buttery yellow to sweeten a summer's evening.

*T*he largest-flowered and one of the state's most beautiful native orchids is yellow lady's slipper. It is also one of the rarest. Several years are required for the plants to produce flowers, and then they can only do so in an older, open forest habitat. Most woodlands are harvested for timber before reaching this age.

PHOTO: GEYATA AJILVSGI

The captivating blossoms of purple pleat-leaf, a member of the iris family, remain open only a short period during the coolness of early morning.

Perhaps the loveliest of the milkweeds, white-flowered milkweed can be found in sandy meadows and sunny borders among the pines.

Right:

In colors ranging from white to rose to deepest blue, hairy spiderwort is one of the earliest wildflowers to bloom. Its first flowers gather in tight clusters at ground level, but as the weather warms, the flowering stalk elongates, eventually holding the blossoms well above the foliage.

*Clasping-leaved coneflower prefers the coolness of
a little extra moisture on its roots and chooses such habitats
as floodplains and slow-draining bar ditches.*

Left:

*Golden wave is aptly named, for in early spring it
covers East Texas's open lands in rippling waves of
purest gold.*

Previous pages:

*While several species of bluebonnets grow in the
state, the Texas bluebonnet — seen here with its frequent
companion, the Indian paintbrush — is the most common.*

Woolly-white, also called wild cauliflower, produces showy, fragrant blooms on solitary plants that form large colonies.

Right:
There is no denying spring's arrival when clumps of blue-eyed grass form spectacular masses of blue or violet on warm, sunny days. Cheery dots of yellow brighten the flowers' centers.

SOUTH TEXAS

SOUTH TEXAS
Coast, prairies, and chaparral

⚜

*P*lovers skim across the wet sand, shuffling their feet and leaning into their stride. Gulls hang against the wind. The shallows of the tide mirror the blues and grays of the outlying ocean and sky. Still inflated and throbbing, sail sacs of the Portuguese man-of-war, a jellyfish with a vicious sting, look like party favors stranded on the sand—royal blue balloons with a rainbow cast. Sand dollars, deceased sea urchins that have been scrubbed clean of life's velvet, lie half-buried in the tidal pools. Gummy tarballs spot the shore, the gift of massive platform oil rigs and fuel tanks of ships flushed at sea. But the warm surf and shifting tugs of the dynamic sand feel good on bare human feet. Though the waves could be grander, and the water prettier, Texas has some of the best walking beaches on earth.

From the Rio Grande to the Sabine, the concave bend of the Gulf Coast extends four hundred miles, and sand barriers shield all but eighty miles of the mainland. When the sea level stabilized in response to the last melting of the Ice Age glaciers, about 5,000 years ago, the barrier islands began to form as submerged sandbars. With the glacial melt, the raised sea backed far up the river valleys, creating large bays. The region's rivers cease to move gravel as their beds lose gradient on the flat coastal plains, and fine clay particles are flushed in suspension through the bays, miles out into the Gulf. Grains of sand meanwhile skip and roll

*B*each morning glories sink their roots deep into the ever-shifting sands.

Previous pages: *B*lossoms of white prickly poppy claim the springtime prairie.

Laguna Madre is a busy spawning ground for fish, clams, and snails, attracting long-legged shorebirds such as the great blue heron.

and, when no longer propelled by the freshwater currents, the quartz particles accrete near the mouths of the streams. Wind and waves then combine to shove the sand back against the mainland. The tides wash in at an angle, creating littoral currents that flow along the shore. All of this deposits the sand in narrow strips.

Beyond the swash zone of the waves, the wind arranges the dry sand in berms, cusps, and dunes. Active dunes continue to shift windward, moving up to thirty yards a year. The vegetation that can stabilize these dunes, and make them permanent, has learned to cope both with chaotic soil conditions and frequent sprays of salt water, ruinous to most plants. Grasses lay much of the stable dunes' foundation—sea oats, coastal dropseed, bitter panicum, seacoast bluestem—but forbs also hold the sand. Railroad vines snake among clumps of silver croton. The flowers of beach evening primrose open late in the afternoon, last through the night, and close just as beach morning glory and goat-foot morning glory present their blooms. Camphor daisies thrive on piles of shell, and in the heat of midday, the blooms of shaggy portulaca spread a purple cloak across the most barren salt flats. Spotted with small ponds and marshes, the vegetation barrier at mid-island—grasses, white milkwort, bright legumes like scarlet pea—can support modest herds of livestock, but ranchers have not stocked the barrier islands with much more restraint than counterparts have shown on the prairies and plains. Near the lagoon that separates the island from the mainland, the rear dunes grow active again, falling toward the wind-tidal flats.

When the barrier islands first formed, they were a chain of short, raised sandbars between the mouths of the rivers, but accretion and the littoral currents gradually closed most of the tidal inlets. Padre Island is thus the largest barrier island along U.S. shores—an uncommon body of land that's 113 miles long and no more than 2.5 miles wide. To its rear, water in Laguna Madre is intensely salty, but grasses, sedges, rushes, and saltworts grow thick in the three-foot shallows—a busy spawning ground for fish, clams, and snails. Long-legged shorebirds step about, stabbing with their beaks.

At some points along the beachless mainland shore, the division of water and prairie resembles a neatly barbered hairline. As the marshes continue inland, the level of salt in the water diminishes but fluctuates in reaction to storm-driven floods. Wildflowers change in corresponding relation to their saline tolerance. Sea oxeye and salt-marsh morning glory flourish along the lagoon, while salt marshmallow, found around tidal pools, spreads inland through marshes of receding brackishness. Coiled in the mud are succulent clumps of seaside heliotrope, with flower spikes that inspired the Spanish name *cola de mico,* or monkey's tail. Its

*The salt marshmallow is found around tidal pools
and spreads inland through marshes of receding
brackishness.*

seeds attract wild ducks. Cattails, with erect, fuzzy brown cylinders, mark the change to freshwater marshes. American germander, lizard's tail, and bluish sheets of mistflower color the soggy inland ground. Yellow cups of water primrose bloom in wide bands and floating mats along the slow-moving channels. Some sloughs are choked with water hyacinth, a troublesome exotic from Brazil that balances its imperial ways with gorgeous, orchidlike flowers.

South Texas weather guarantees a luxuriant wildflower habitat. Although the winter northers shift the wind around and combine with the humidity for biting chill factors, at Corpus Christi temperatures reach freezing only ten days a year. At the lower end of Padre Island, the average temperature is a balmy 74°. Many wildflower species bloom throughout the year. Considering the inundated state of much of its terrain, the southern Gulf Coast has surprisingly moderate rainfall, averaging 26–29 inches annually. But due to the cyclonic storms that swirl in from the Gulf, ten inches often come in one cloudburst. The viviparous seeds of the black mangrove shrub, a tropical species, can either take root where they fall or float till they find ground. Another resourceful plant, the aromatic camphor weed, can bloom in marshy soil that is soaked with fresh water one month, brine the next. On an average of two times every three years, tropical storms turn into hurricanes, which wreak havoc on both the tenuous construction of the barrier islands and the delicate equilibrium of the marshes. Tropical storms qualify as hurricanes when wind velocities reach 74 miles an hour. This is an arbitrary figure, but since that's roughly the wind speed required to lift an adult human off his or her feet, the estimate will do.

When the Gulf hurled a storm-battered raft commanded by Álvar Núñez Cabeza de Vaca on Galveston Beach in 1527, the Spaniards named the place Malhado, the Island of Doom. Resident Indians, whom they called Capoques and Han, first made them medicine men (as best they could, they practiced the Christian art of faith-healing) and then abused them as slaves. Although the aborigines trapped a few fish in cane weirs, they mostly grubbed for nutty roots in tidal shoals—at great cost to the fingers of women. On the mainland in spring, they subsisted on blackberries and oysters. As the other Spaniards died, Cabeza de Vaca saw that he had to escape the coast. Trying to reach settlements in Mexico, he wandered for a decade as a trader among inland tribes. In later centuries, fierce, tattooed Karankawas dominated the coast from Galveston to north Padre, while Coahuiltecans camped along central and lower Padre to the Rio Grande. These tribes summered on the barrier islands and crossed the lagoons when the northers came. They fished, hunted deer and birds, and harvested the fruits of cactus. They

*F*orming low, creeping mats on the sands of bay and island beaches, cenicilla opens small, five-petaled stars among succulent foliage — each rosy-pink petal tipped with green.

Opposite page:
*D*espite its gorgeous flowers, water hyacinth remains a troublesome exotic that chokes many East Texas waterways as well as coastal sloughs of South Texas.

PHOTO: STEPHAN MYERS

The brilliant blooms of Drummond phlox turn entire pastures bright red in earliest spring.

ate alligator meat and, to repel mosquitoes, smeared themselves with the reptiles' vile, acrid oil.

Man has not always thrived in this habitat, and periodically, the hurricanes still clear the shore of beer joints and bait camps, even beach-front condominiums. But it's a wonderland for birds. Wedge formations of migrating geese, swans, and pelicans adorn the coastal sky. Creation of the marshland Aransas National Wildlife Refuge saved whooping cranes from extinction, and the Nature Conservancy has recently enlarged the flock's protected winter range through purchase of the southern tip of Matagorda Island. From Laguna Atascosa to Anahuac, four more national wildlife refuges are strung along the mainland coast, the Texas Fish and Wildlife Service manages large tracts on behalf of the state, and the Padre Island National Seashore protects teeming rookeries on islets in Laguna Madre. In early spring, while mockingbirds establish jealous territories and assail robins and cardinals, migrants from Mexico's Yucatan Peninsula take a shortcut over the Gulf: warblers, finches, buntings, sparrows, nighthawks. Dawns in the marshes ignite a tumultuous, ongoing screech.

⚜

The marshlands gradually yield to a curving promontory of the state's central prairies and savannahs. The woodland patterns change south-ward, along the coast, from the Houston area's sugarberries and longleaf pines to large pecans, elms, and live oaks around Victoria and Goliad. Farther inland, hickories and post oaks surround detached fingers of the blackland prairie. The savannah's division of grassland and forest tends to be abrupt; trees stand bunched together in mottes. "These islands are one of the most enchanting features of Texas scenery," one early settler wrote. "They are to be found in all shapes—circular, parallel-ograms, hexagons, octagons—some again twisting and winding like dark green snakes over the brighter surface of the prairie."

Indiangrass and little bluestem dominate the virgin coastal prairie, and with more rain and less cold weather, the native wildflower habitat resembles and even transcends that of the central tall-grass regions. But the rich clay and sandy loam soils have likewise incurred the fate of the other grasslands. The suburban sprawl of Houston has bulldozed and paved over a great chunk of good floral range. Fields on the flat coastal plain are plowed within a few yards of farmhouse walls, and while South Texas contains an exemplar of well-heeled range management, the vast King Ranch, overgrazing has changed the region's assertive vegetation from tall and midgrasses to Macartney rose and Chinese tallow—shrubby exotics—and mesquite and huisache, the native woody invaders.

But the coastal grassland still offers some of the state's most extravagant floral panoramas. Drummond phlox and field pansies turn pastures bright

*P*hlox and coreopsis weave a tapestry of glowing
reds and yellows across the early spring landscape
of southern Texas.

Twine vine, a member of the milkweed family, drapes beautiful balls of pink and white across fences and low shrubbery.

Opposite page:
Across open prairies and in rocky limestone soils, Arkansas yucca raises tall spikes of drooping, creamy bells.

red and blue as early as February. Along with the rainbow array of bluebonnets, Indian paintbrush, coreopsis, Indian blanket, plains wild indigo, butterweed, and Mexican hat, hundreds of acres of the ranches are whitened by false garlic, Philadelphia fleabane, and snow-on-the-prairie. Bright yellow fringed puccoon and low hop clover, a soil-building but weedy exotic, line the edges of the woods and fill the meadows. Baby blue-eyes and violet wood-sorrel seek the company of live oaks. Prairie phlox follows the fencerows, rose prickly poppy accepts the depleted soil, and beautiful false dragonhead congregates in the roadside bar ditches. At the peak of spring wildflower season, pilots of small planes look for reasons to fly over the King Ranch.

South of Baffin Bay, the prairie loams change into a drier sand plain. West of the caliche Bordas Escarpment, annual rainfall tails off to an arid 18 inches. The vegetative zones of Central, South, and West Texas merge among the mesas and two-hundred-foot cliffs of the Devil's River, which heads on the Edwards Plateau in Sutton County and empties into the Rio Grande at Lake Amistad. Lined with sycamores and pecans, the Devil's River is the state's last major unpolluted stream. Above the transparent cascades of Dolan Falls, 22,000 gallons a minute gush from the hillside springs. But inland from the coast, as far north as San Antonio, and west to Devil's River, the brush country, or the chaparral, has the look and feel of dusty northern Mexico.

The word chaparral came into Spanish by means of the ancient language of the Basques. It referred to thickets of short evergreen oaks on the foothills and plateaus of the Basques' homeland Pyrenees. In English, chaparral has taken a broader meaning: "a dense impenetrable thicket of shrubs or dwarf trees." Another telling word has roots in the same etymology: chaps, the leather leggings that protect horsemen from the scrapes and punctures of thorns.

South Texas's first cowboys spoke Spanish. They tied iron stakes to their saddles and drove them in the ground when they dismounted. Otherwise, they said, they had no way to tether their horses. Tall sabal palms lined the lower Rio Grande, and there were mottes of Texas palmetto and Texas ebony, but the early *vaqueros* navigated the uniform grassland like sailors—they learned the stars. Though grass was plentiful, rain was not. The overgrazing of Texas began in the chaparral. Tamaulipan thorn shrubs first took advantage of the depleted prairies, and the dwarf oaks soon dwelt in the crowded shade of huisache and mesquite. Early maps of the Anglo settlers simply designated the region "Wild Horses." Along with the mustang herds, Mexican cattle roamed the brush range freely. The *vaqueros* rounded them up infrequently, as best they could. Lank, mean, and resourceful, longhorns thrived in this habitat and developed as the hallowed frontier breed.

A small jumping spider, dwarfed by the petal of a prickly pear, waits in anticipation of a meal.

Some of the region's succulents—prickly pear, sotol, desert Christmas cactus, yucca in tall feathery bloom, agave with floral stalks which look like giant spears of asparagus—range far across the state, but black lace cactus and Runyon's cory cactus appear only in the Rio Grande plain. Rattlesnakes are not the least of the hazards that puncture the human leg. Still, the chaparral of the lower Valley does not have the eerie menace of the deserts north and west. The mouth of the Rio Grande is only 180 miles north of the Tropic of Cancer, and the sheer number of plant species increases in relative proximity to the tropics. (Panama has about 7,500 native species, for example, while temperate Austria, the same size, claims 2,300.)

Bastardia, a mallow native to South and Central America, reaches its northern limit in the Rio Grande Valley. Muted reds of peonía and bracted sida cluster in the brush. Set against silver leaves, *tulipán del monte* blooms crimson throughout the year. Butterflies and hummingbirds hover over red flower whorls of tropical sage. Pink mint colors the shaded brush. Wildlife eat the seeds of Lindheimer tephrosia, a graceful legume with purplish-rose petals. Even on the driest tracts, dwarf dalea lightens the stark ground with shows of bright yellow. Colonies of blue-eyed grass look like shallow lakes.

Flying lazily about on silver-spangled wings, the Gulf fritillary spends warm summer days nectaring on such favored food sources as the Texas thistle.

Opposite page:
Amelia's sand-verbena blankets deep, barren sands with large, fragrant clusters of purple to rose-pink flowers in spring and early summer.

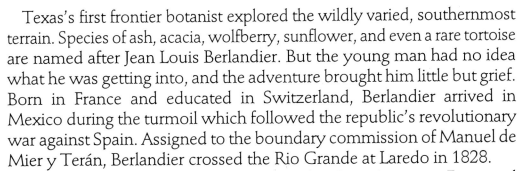

The fox squirrel prefers a rather open habitat in hardwood forests or in mixed hardwoods and pines. These squirrels spend much time scampering about among tree branches with no object apparent other than fun.

Texas's first frontier botanist explored the wildly varied, southernmost terrain. Species of ash, acacia, wolfberry, sunflower, and even a rare tortoise are named after Jean Louis Berlandier. But the young man had no idea what he was getting into, and the adventure brought him little but grief. Born in France and educated in Switzerland, Berlandier arrived in Mexico during the turmoil which followed the republic's revolutionary war against Spain. Assigned to the boundary commission of Manuel de Mier y Terán, Berlandier crossed the Rio Grande at Laredo in 1828.

He collected enthusiastically along the San Antonio, Frio, and Guadalupe rivers. But horse thieves subjected him to a ten-mile walk; spring downpours and leaky tents ruined his specimens; crossings of the flood-swollen streams were horrendous; and he caught malaria from the mosquitoes. "He sent some dried plants in small number, badly chosen, and badly prepared," an uncharitable professor in Geneva dismissed his student, citing an expenditure of 16,000 francs. Berlandier married a Mexican woman and became a pharmacist and physician in the Tamaulipan border town of Matamoros. He drowned while trying to cross another flooded river in 1851.

Five and a half centuries ago, Cabeza de Vaca knew the Rio Grande as Rio de Palmas, River of Palms. Today, the National Audubon Society manages the last large stand of native sabal palms, and that grove, south of Brownsville, covers only 35 acres. The sentinel palms that line the highways are exotics from Mexico, and their importation placed them beyond their safe natural range. Rare cold snaps strip the fronds and leave dead trunks arrayed like rows of warped utility poles. In 1899, Texas's worst norther on record plunged temperatures in the Valley to 12°. These days, freezes are considered an ecological disaster because they kill the citrus trees. The fertile topsoil in the river valley goes as deep as 60 feet, and irrigation has transformed the terrain yet again, this time with cultivated vegetation—red grapefruit, sugar cane, parsley, mustard greens, okra. On unplowed tracts, most ranchers clear the brush with hopes of improving the grassland. All these layers and loops of change have created environmental irony: thickened by land abuse in prior centuries, the chaparral of the lower Valley has become one of Texas's most endangered and valued natural habitats. The surviving patches are easy to see from the air. They're distinctly greener.

With plans of transferring the preserve to the state, the Nature Conservancy recently purchased part of the Schalaben Ranch west of Raymondville. A few keepsake longhorns still roam the place. The spotted beasts look incongruous in their historic range; when they turn their heads, their horns snag brush. Longhorns must have developed very

*L*emon horsemint

A paper wasp visits the florets of salt cedar
looking for a meal, be it some small caterpillar or
nectar from the flowers.

strong necks. With antlers that make the feat all the more impressive, a surprised whitetail buck ducks neatly and fast under the lower strand of a barbed wire fence, then flees into the thicket. No more desirous of human company, a black javelina, the chaparral's wild pig, scuttles off in its ungainly, low-hipped stride. Coyotes stammer and yip a few yards off in the brush—one of the happiest sounds in nature. Harris hawks cruise just above the trees. Footprints of raccoons and bobcats mark the mud around a stock tank. Ocelots, spotted jungle cats, have been tracked on the well-preserved ranch. Mockingbirds cut through the briar patch, followed by the spectacular swoop of a blue-headed and yellow-tailed green jay, whose range extends from Bolivia to Texas's southernmost tip.

But the Nature Conservancy desired this site for the wealth of its flora, not the fauna. Spring has come to the Valley the first week of March. Mesquites are gnarled trees wherever they appear, but here they grow thick-trunked and impressive. Their lime green foliage filters the slanting afternoon light. Naked, thorny, and inelegant a week ago, the huisache shrubs and trees glow now in goldish orange bloom. Huisache flowers are delicate balls of fluff, about the size of a dime. The silvery foliage of cenizo, or purple sage, has begun to show its violet blooms. Not a true sage, the shrub belongs to the family of penstemons and snapdragons. Farther south, in Mexico, a cool splash of rain on hot days turns hillsides solid purple with blooming cenizo.

Weedy but pretty, lantana presents its multicolored clusters around clumps of prickly pear and along the fences. Closer to the ground, parralena and dwarf dandelion match brilliant yellows side by side. The edges of the chaparral are given to colonies of purple phacelia, which may be the state's most under-appreciated spring flower. The west side of the Schalaben Ranch looks across plowed fields at a salt lake which Spain claimed in 1746 with the explanation that salt was money, and all of nature's money belonged to the crown. Hence the name of the lake, El Sal del Rey, the Salt of the King. This day, the view from the chaparral bolsters a sense of the tropics: the perfect round ember, hanging on the horizon rim, of a pink and mauve sundown.

A great Southern white butterfly seeks nectar from the clustered golden blossoms of lantana.

Opposite page:
*I*ts trusses of golden-yellow constantly tossed about by sea breezes, seaside goldenrod forms tall clumps in coastal swales and depressions.

*I*ndifferent to the salt and sea air, Texas
prickly pear forms large, sprawling clumps across
coastal sands.

The blossoms of Texas prickly pear may vary from pale yellow to burnt orange. Deeply cupped, thick-textured petals surround numerous pollen-laden stamens.

Low-growing and often hidden by surrounding grasses, horse crippler is a cactus to be reckoned with. If stepped on, its fiercely strong spines can cause great pain to man or beast.

Right:
Petals of purest rose form large flowers of the pitaya, one of the cacti scattered across eroded saline sands along Boca Chica Road, at the southernmost tip of the state.

Tornillo, or dwarf screw bean, hugs the ground
and is easily overlooked. In spring its ferny foliage
supports small balls of fuzzy yellow flowers that are
followed by tightly and spirally coiled fruits.

*F*rom the shallow banks of streams or ponds,
water-primrose edges waterward in low,
floating mats.

*T*he small flower clusters of beach pimpernel nestle
among leathery foliage on plants favoring moist
soils along the banks of ponds, streams, or
roadside ditches.

Right:
*L*ike miniature yellow candles, flowering spikes of
queen's delight rise above already-formed
seed capsules.

*L*indheimer tephrosia is an especially beautiful
legume of well-drained sands, opening large, showy
flowers in long racemes throughout the season.

Agarito, a coastal Oxalis, competes with grasses
and brushy undergrowth in scattered chaparral or
in the semishade of live oak mottes.

*S*atiny white blossoms of cluster cordia open
half-hidden in the semishade of brush and
woodland edges.

Right:
*D*awn in the chaparral of South Texas finds a
yellow water lily opening on the surface of a
still pond.

Tropical sage is a plant of many habitats, being equally at home in moist, sandy soils, chaparral brushlands, or on limestone cliffs.

Right:

A tree of many common names, retama bears large clusters of beautiful red and yellow flowers during hot summer months, providing nectar and pollen for a host of insects.

In twin coiled racemes, seaside heliotrope slowly
unrolls dainty white or bluish flowers. This
common plant of beaches and salt flats produces
clumps of succulent, bluish-green foliage.

Right:
*E*xquisite tiny blossoms of creamy white twisted
into slender spirals easily identify spring ladies'
tresses, a common native orchid of the
coastal sands.

*A*nacahuita, or wild olive, bears lovely white
flowers in short clusters. The handsome
ornamental shrub or small tree is used in
cultivation but readily escapes to fencerows and dry
creek beds.

Left:
*T*exas palafoxia is abundant in some coastal
areas, often on beach shell. Opening first flowers in
April, it may continue to bloom through December.

*Brilliant red blossoms of tulipán del monte
nestle among silvery, heart-shaped leaves, creating
a striking display.*

Left:
*Preferring a moist habitat, hierba del cancer
stands with feet in the water of roadside ditches
and shallow edges of marshes.*

*S*prawling in moist swales, ditches, and other
low places, globe amaranth produces numerous
round heads of pink to purple-rose flowers.

*A*n aromatic, thorny, evergreen shrub of
chaparral country, lime prickly ash in early spring
puts forth numerous clusters of orange-scented
flowers on its zigzag branches.

*W*ith roots deeply imbedded in wet, saline
soils, sea oxeye produces a mass of stiff, hard,
sunflower-like blooms.

Right:
*F*lowering stems of Buckley yucca appear too
small to bear the large, loose panicles of creamy
bells. Yucca flowers are the only larval food source
of the lovely, snow-white yucca moth.

The spirally twisted petals of Drummond wax mallow never fully open. Later the plants produce an edible fruit resembling tiny apples.

*F*orming clusters of salmon-colored spikes, scarlet
pea sprawls low to the ground in sandy soils of
beach and prairie.

*T*he plentiful nectar produced by Amelia's sand-
verbena attracts many species of butterflies,
including the beautiful giant swallowtail.

*B*luish clumps of coastal mistflower color areas of
soggy inland ground where the salinity has
diminished somewhat.

Tiny yellow blossoms speckled with maroon cluster in whorls beneath the pale lavender bracts of spotted beebalm. The noticeably aromatic plants often form extensive stands.

Right:

Seeking shade and moisture, false dayflower opens its two-petaled flower for only a short period in early mornings. The third petal of this flower never fully develops and remains minute and inconspicuous.

NORTH TEXAS

NORTH TEXAS
Rolling and high plains

⚜

*I*n March of 1852, an Army captain named Randolph Marcy received orders to find the source of the Red River. In Marcy's words, the North Texas plains that the river crossed were still *"terra incognita,"* an unknown land. Marcy was a precise cartographer, an accomplished illustrator, and in later years, a successful author—one of the gentlemen officers who advanced scientific knowledge of the American West. As a scientist, Marcy's own interests ran toward zoology, but his thorough and ably written account also included reports and tables on geology, meteorology, fossils, Indian languages, and a list of two hundred plants that he collected, preserved, and shipped to a botanist in New York. As dutifully as he watched the horizon for hostile Comanches, the career soldier stooped and picked wildflowers along the way.

At a bivouac that spring in the granite Wichita Mountains of southern Oklahoma, Marcy wrote in his journal that one expanse of grass and wildflowers was the prettiest valley he had ever seen. Working down toward Texas, he explored post-oak woods and a network of creeks, logging dates on which he collected stiff-stem flax and Engelmann daisies. But a band of Wichita Indians told the captain that his mission up Red River entailed a hard eighteen-day ride which they did not recommend. Infants died from drinking the brackish river water, they said, and adults died of thirst when they abandoned the plains' foul-tasting streams. The locations of potable springs were properties of mystical instinct and

*T*eucrium *forms thick colonies in low areas where the infrequent rains collect.*

Previous pages: C*lumps of yellow-flowered day-primrose in Cap Rock country.*

Although locoweed or crazy weed is one of the more toxic plants of the plains country, the spikes of lavender to purple flowers are exceptionally beautiful. The clumps often grow along road cuts or on rocky, deeply eroded slopes.

desperate conjecture. The higher Staked Plains, or *llano estacado*, lay beyond the western horizon. Marcy had been told that the high plains took their Spanish name from New Mexicans who drove stakes in the ground, trying to plot a route between water holes.

With erosive rivers and creeks cutting through red Permian clay, the lower rolling plains contained luxuriant stretches of midgrass prairie. They were tufted with little bluestem and blue and sideoats grama and colored with wild blue indigo, plains poppy mallow, wine-cup, coreopsis, Mexican hat, plains daisy, and two-leaved senna. Mesquite trees had not yet choked the grassland into submission. Before the great cattle drives and subsequent overstocking of the range, frontiersmen associated mesquites with nearby water. They knew that wild horses ate the beans and by digestive process distributed the seeds, and they believed the mustangs rarely browsed more than three miles from water. Marcy worked back and forth across the Red River, ranging miles from its broad sandy bed. He gathered specimens of mustang grape, crameria, small palafoxia, prairie phlox, and Arkansas lazy daisy. But then the breaks and divides of the plains rivers would abruptly deteriorate into desolate badlands growing little but cactus. Crossing the badlands of the Wichita River, the soldiers' animals bled from the bites of horse-flies which Marcy claimed were the size of hummingbirds.

White strata in the naked red clay resembled limestone, but the material was gypsum. Dissolved in water and ingested by humans unaccustomed to the chemistry, gypsum salts have the effect of Epsom salts. The Army calculated that Texas's surface gypsum deposits fouled drinking water in a belt three hundred miles long, north to south, and fifty to one hundred miles across. Also fearing scurvy, Marcy rejoiced in mid-June when they came upon a sand hill abloom with wild onion—they all needed the vitamins of fresh vegetables. Suffering the purgative water and rubber flasks which made it taste even worse, the soldiers began the daily march at three in the morning and quit the heat before noon, so the horses, mules, and oxen could graze. Some of the forage was hazardous. The poisonous plains paper-flower thrives on gypsum soil; more dangerous is the highly toxic and eagerly grazed locoweed. The soldiers' Eastern-bred horses were terrified of buffalo. To keep Indians from stealing the animals, the soldiers drove them back into camp and guarded them closely at night. Over the summer, the company was erroneously reported massacred by Comanches. The War Department passed on this report to Marcy's family, who donned clothes of mourning. A minister preached his funeral sermon.

Meanwhile, Marcy picked white prickly poppy, Indian blanket, Dakota vervain, Indian rush-pea, pink plains penstemon, and fragrant,

*A*ncient, gnarled juniper trees cling tenaciously to
a rocky outcropping above Palo Duro Canyon
State Park.

Clinging to steep canyon walls, Missouri primrose opens wide yellow blossoms to the sun's early warmth.

Plains zinnia forms ground-hugging cushions of bright yellow flowers, covering mesas, slopes, and roadsides.

evening-blooming scarlet gaura. After exploring each of the Red's upper tributaries and forks, Marcy correctly decided that the Prairie Dog Town Fork was the headwater stream. As they penetrated the Texas Panhandle, temperatures reached 104°. Distances undulated with heat mirages. Watching the phantom lakes, Marcy recalled the deluded accounts of French soldiers who thought they marched toward water during Napoleon's invasion of Egypt.

By now, the soldiers stayed close to the shallow twining river. Groves of cottonwoods lined the Red's banks. Plains Indians invested cottonwoods with almost spiritual mystique; for one thing, when snow buried the prairies, their horses would eat the trees' sweet bark. "The atmosphere," Marcy wrote one night, "is redolent with the delightful perfume which is emitted from their blossoms." The cottonwood's slick, heart-shaped leaves clatter like those of its mountain relative, the aspen, and give the high plains their best fall color. Found near water, cottonwoods are oasis trees. But this water made the men sick. Constant wind turned the river bottom into a columnar dust storm by midafternoon. Horses staggered in the soft, rodent-burrowed earth of the dry banks, and the riders reined them around wet spots that looked firm but might be quicksand—a condition created by upward-flowing groundwater which holds soil particles in suspension. A flash flood chased the soldiers to higher ground three days after they had seen the last rain. The Delaware Indian guides assured them it was a good omen.

At the end of June, Marcy halted the wagons and proceeded with pack mules, saddle horses, and fewer men. The bluestem and gramas had begun to change to drought-withered buffalo grass; they were passing from midgrass prairie into the higher and dryer short-grass plains. As the bluffs along the river grew in height, Marcy commented on the beauty of the gleaming gypsum strata. Then, suddenly, they were staring at five-hundred-foot rock cliffs that shaded upward in maroon, lavender, olive, gray, yellow, and beige. Woods of red juniper somehow found enough soil to root in nearly vertical array. Mealy sage, plains blackfoot, and Missouri primrose bloomed on the canyon walls. Marked by a dramatic escarpment called the Cap Rock, a southern promontory of the Great Plains covers most of the Texas Panhandle. Marcy viewed the escarpment from the floor of Palo Duro Canyon, a fabulous chasm that began as a simple erosion gully a million years ago. The canyon floor was covered with thick prairie. Marcy added goat's rue, spectacle-pod, and plains zinnia to his collection of wildflowers. Here the soldiers found a riverbed of gravel, not sand. They must have fallen on their faces in the sweet, spring-fed water.

Marcy can be forgiven for not pursuing a network of intermittent creeks and flash-flood draws to the Red's true, if technical, source on the

Scattered amid the thin grasslands of the rolling plains, day-primrose forms low mounds of bright color.

Cornflowers

plains of New Mexico. They might not have survived the rest of the adventure. On July 4, the soldiers celebrated Independence Day by starting home. That day they found a round pool of clear water thirty feet deep and eighty yards across. The boulders, crags, and mesas of Palo Duro Canyon drove Marcy to the far reaches of his Romantic prose style:

> Occasionally might be seen a good representation of the towering walls of a castle of the feudal ages, with its giddy battlements pierced with loopholes.... Then again, our fancy pictured a colossal specimen of sculpture, representing the human figure, with all the features of the face distinctly defined. This, standing upon its pedestal, overlooks the valley, as if it had been designed and executed by the Almighty Artist as the presiding genius of these dismal solitudes.

❧

The work of the frontier naturalists has been inherited by people who, by necessity, approach the task as plant conservationists. Benny Simpson, for example, grew up on a small cattle ranch and grain farm south of Childress, where, both in latitude and longitude, the Panhandle begins. Simpson studied agronomy and farm instruments at Texas Tech, but that was during the long and disastrous drought of the 1950s. He became a plant collector and researcher for the Texas A&M Agricultural Experiment Station at Dallas because he wasn't confident the home place could operate much longer. One century after Randolph Marcy's passing, the North Texas plains were worn out.

In recent years, plant conservationists in Texas looked for direction to an amiable triumvirate composed of Simpson and two cohorts: Lynn Lowrey, an East Texas nurseryman who would disappear happily and frequently on plant-collecting expeditions in Mexico, and Carroll Abbott, a dropout politico who had moved home to Comfort and grown a beard. In his former guise, Abbott wrote speeches and maneuvered behind the scenes for Lyndon Johnson. He was the man behind the packets of bluebonnet seeds that John Connally mailed constituents as Texas governor. As the Johnny Appleseed of Texas wildflowers, Abbott was often found in bar ditches, gathering seeds in grocery sacks. Ill health claimed him before he could realize the dream of his company, Green Horizons. His death in 1984 deeply saddened his friends.

"Carroll used to park his pickup and sell seeds by the side of the road," Simpson reminisced. "One day a man turned around and came back and gave him a thousand dollars. 'I like what you're doing,' he said, then drove off again. I don't think he even told Carroll his name. But that wasn't the usual feedback. The three of us just gravitated together.

The spectacular Palo Duro Canyon, its dramatic escarpment a blend of color, began as a simple erosion gully over a million years ago.

Following pages:
Multihued cornflowers await the approach of a summer storm on the open plain.

*E*agerly grazed by livestock, clumps of Engelmann daisy like this one are becoming harder to find.

Opposite page:

*O*nce called "Indian sun," annual sunflower is a many-branched plant that can reach as high as fourteen feet in one season, with each branch bearing an impressive disk of brown and gold.

Looking for somebody to talk to, I suppose. For a long time, people would ask, 'And what do you do?' 'Oh, I'm into native plants…wildflowers.' 'Very interesting,' they'd say, and go way up on their toes, looking on to far parts of the room."

With a ruddy, round face and extended white sideburns, Simpson resembles the comedian W.C. Fields, in a straw cowboy hat. "We came into this country as conquerors," he said. "And we've just about conquered it out of existence. Most of the botanizing of Texas gets done in bar ditches. On roadsides, the plants at least have a chance—now that the highway department doesn't have quite so much budget for mowing. Inside the fences, the habitat has either been plowed up or grazed to the ground. What's prettier than Engelmann daisies? But they're hard to find now. The livestock eat them all."

"And we're running out of water," he went on. "Every drop we have is overcommitted. We can't go on watering lawns and flower beds in the cities the way we do now. We need ornamental plants that can withstand our weather conditions. To introduce species, you first look for the same general latitude. But introductions from Florida, Arizona, and California have a hard time here because our winters are colder. And exotics aren't the answer. The closest equivalents to the Texas habitat are in Afghanistan, Iran, and the pampas of Argentina. Now, given the politics, what American's going to hunt for plants in those countries?"

"Plus, exotics are so unpredictable. Some little check and balance in the native range is always missing in the new environment. Australians wish they'd never seen our scenic cactus. One of our worst weeds, Johnson grass, was supposed to be a Turkish wonder forage a century ago. Bermuda grass, which came from Africa, has adapted so well it's almost native, but the lawn varieties need sprinklers to get through an ordinary Texas summer. So maybe we ought to try buffalo grass, which has coped with droughts on the plains for thousands of years. Personally, I like woody plants and wildflowers. I'm in the business of finding attractive and beneficial native plants that can do without all that moisture; maybe Texas A&M can get a grant to study vegetation that's drought-resistant. There's no federal money available to research a plant because it's lovely, or because it uplifts the soul."

⚜

The Texas Panhandle gets only 16–20 inches of rain a year. It's also the coldest part of the state. While the mean annual temperature in southernmost Texas is 74°, in the Panhandle's northwest corner the average reading is a cool 56°. Subzero temperatures are expected of the winters; snowstorms are celebrated elsewhere in Texas as pretty and frolicsome novelties, but on the high plains they can turn into killer blizzards.

Spring does not fully arrive until the first of May. The wind blows constantly, and for miles in all directions, nothing grows much higher than yucca, prairie larkspur, blue gilia, pale trumpets, and evening primroses. The sameness of the plains had the first Europeans who crossed them wandering in loops. Randolph Marcy informed governmental officials in Washington that the high plains of Texas were uninhabitable. By reputation, the *llano estacado* was a place of madness, thirst, and terror.

But the solitudes were not so dismal after all: the explorer Marcy helped disprove his own vision of the region's future. As soon as the Army defeated the last Comanches and windmill-driven wells tapped the underground source of water, the high plains filled up with ranchers and farmers. They did not have to dwell in cavelike dugouts or sod houses made from the turf of buffalo grass. And the low mesas and endless stretches of pale green terrain have a hypnotic kind of charm. When spring finally comes to the short-grass plains, the dearth of trees emphasizes the abundance of wildflowers. Dune bluebonnets, the state's rarest species, appear only in the northwest corner of the Panhandle. Their range extends through New Mexico and the Oklahoma Panhandle— high prairies that arrive at the slopes of the Rocky Mountains. The Rockies can't be seen from the Texas Panhandle, but a sense of their nearness is carried, even in summer, by the coolness in the air.

An extravagant, bushy perennial that covers itself with bright yellow flowers and woolly leaves, plains paper-flower is a common inhabitant of the high plains. Blooms remain on the plant for months, the yellows slowly fading to pale browns and tans, and the petals becoming crisp and papery.

*The lavender blooms of salt cedar line the banks
of the Brazos River.*

*Overlooking a gypsum-
tainted stream, plains
blackfoot forms mounds of
delightful white daisies.*

Locoweed

Accustomed to dry and barren ground, gold spikes of Fendler bladderpod are among the first spring flowers. Plains yellow daisy also favors dry and chalky soils. Elsewhere, intermittent springs seep laterally and create lush meadows called vegas; butterweed responds with solid acres of gold. Rainwater collects in shallow, evaporative lakes called playas. Catchment basins with no inlet or exit streams, the playa lakes are regular and almost crowded features of this strange ongoing plain. Seldom more than a mile apart, the playas' water-conditioned beds nurture colonies of arrowhead, knotweed, and annual aster. For centuries, bison herds rolled in the mud of smaller depressions and wore the sinks deeper. Known as buffalo wallows, these depressions look like sunken bathtubs from the air. At ground level, they're recognized by distinctive yellow flowers—Jones selenia and buffalo bur. Throughout the summer, lemon-scented pectis assembles solid yellow stands on the short-grass prairie. The lemon fragrance of the foliage is so strong that the plants are sometimes smelled before they are seen.

Unfortunately, recreational access is scarce on the high plains. The state sold off its public lands long ago, and state parks tend to be positioned near large population centers. Of 121 state parks, historic sites, and recreational areas, only four are located in the Panhandle. Westward from the large and well-furnished Palo Duro Canyon State Park, the narrower, wilder, and more spectacular canyon is legally fenced off in private ranches—posted against trespassers—because the upstream river and creek beds are piles of dry rocks. But the Panhandle has another major river, the Canadian. It flows across the entire Panhandle before it bends north toward the parent Arkansas River. And in a quirky legacy of Spanish-era law, because of that continual flow the Canadian qualifies in Texas as a navigable stream, even though its water regularly runs no more than shin-deep. West of Lake Meredith, the legal fencing limits of the ranchers open up a continuous valley that stretches up to a mile across. The isolated Canadian Breaks are a hard hike for backpackers, who have to carry drinking water. But as long as horseback riders stay within the barb-wire fences, the highway bridges open gates for them into a little-known wilderness of quasi-public land.

The Canadian Valley was prime buffalo range, the domain of the last free Comanches. Charles Goodnight, the Panhandle's pioneer rancher, said the grasses grew well up beside his saddle when he first rode the Canadian bottoms. Now the dominant tall growth is salt cedar, which has a pleasant fragrance and a frail lavender bloom. Mules like to browse the green shoots. But to botanists, salt cedar is another woody invader, a rampant exotic from Asia. Red junipers cluster in the valley's

*A*long almost every watercourse in the plains, the
dominant tall growth is salt cedar. An aggressive
intruder rather than a native tree, salt cedar
nevertheless carries a pleasant fragrance and
pretty lavender blooms.

Thousands of sunflowers greet the dawn in a mountain meadow. Throughout the day, the stalks will slowly twist and turn, allowing the flowers always to face the sun.

rocky canyons. Mesquite thickets have crowded into the bottom. Beyond the fences, Herefords drink from metal tanks below whirring windmills. The average wind velocity in the Canadian Valley is sixteen miles an hour. Many days, the breeze triples that.

In harnessing that considerable resource, the windmills made the *llano estacado* more inhabitable. After a consecutive drought and record blizzard devastated the cattle industry in 1886, landowners in the Panhandle increasingly turned to farming, and pumped groundwater enhanced their prospects with irrigation. But the wells lowered the table of an aquifer that does not replenish itself, and the warm summers and strong wind evaporate rainwater quickly. All across the Great Plains, over-grazed and eroded grassland awaited the severe drought that coincided with the Depression, and in the farming regions, the topsoil was tilled to exhaustion. By the mid-thirties, thirty-five million acres of American land had deteriorated to the point they could no longer grow crops. Most of rural Texas suffered that ecological disaster, but only the high plains saw the red and black clouds of the Dust Bowl.

In a bit of scientific understatement, "disturbed" is the word applied to much of our soil inheritance. Even in the relatively untrampled Canadian Breaks, the tracks of man can be seen in the vegetation. Vines of buffalo gourd, often mistaken for its watermelon cousin, entwine the mesquite posts of the barb-wire fences. Colonies of wind-pollinated snake-cotton take on a silver sheen in moonlight. Tansy aster and prairie spiderwort paint the hard-scrabble terrain with violet. Clumps of purple ground-cherry thrive on barren ground in conditions of extreme drought. Even the scavenger plants flower. The umbrella shapes and tiny flowers of broomweed—the last resource of topsoil trying to hold itself together —cover the dust with airy hummocks of yellow. Sunflowers, an essential food of birds and deer and a versatile medicine of primitive man, stand six feet tall in the high plains' overgrazed pastures. Throughout the day, their stalks slowly twist and turn, allowing the flowers always to face the life-giving sun.

Braving the fierce winds of May that sweep across the flatlands, plains larkspur sends graceful spires of palest blue above first greening grasses.

*I*n a land dominated by silence and space, plains
prickly pear forms large, spiny thickets penetrable
only by rattlesnakes, desert rats, and armadillos.

*W*estern horse nettle is a tough,
unyielding plant, one of the few remaining in
heavily overgrazed pastures and along frequently
disturbed roadsides.

*The yellow, trumpet-shaped flowers of buffalo gourd
are typical of the gourd family, which
includes squashes, pumpkins, melons,
and cucumbers.*

Right:

*Conspicuous along roadsides, railroad tracks,
and in pastures, buffalo gourd is a striking plant
with long, radiating vines and malodorous foliage.*

*R*ising above the short, thin grasses of the plains, spiny star cactus opens delicate, almost translucent pink petals around the rim of its spiny base.

Right:
*L*ovely to look at but painful to touch, the blossoms of spiny star cactus nestle close within their thorny protection.

*S*everal species of locoweed, or milk-vetch, occur in
Texas. Creamy locoweed bears large, showy spikes
well above a mound of dark-green foliage.

*T*hin vines of globe berry trail over low shrubbery
or into cedar trees, usually in short grass—mesquite
pastures. Yellow, starlike flowers are followed in late
summer by small, roundish, bright-red
gourd-like fruits.

In April and May, teucrium opens oddly shaped white flowers, all of them clustered toward the top of ferny stems.

A covering of soft hairs on the herbage of plains paper-flower enables the plant to survive the severe droughts common to the plains, by reducing the amount of moisture lost to evaporation.

A conspicuous plant of open plains and mesas,
trailing four o'clock spreads slender stems along
dry, sandy terrain, the sticky foliage often covered
with grains of sand.

Right:

*N*o matter how harsh the terrain, square-bud day-
primrose is a tough plant that will find a bit of soil
in which to grow. The showy yellow flowers remain
open during the day, unlike those of the evening
primrose, a close relative.

WEST TEXAS

WEST TEXAS
Mountains and deserts

⚓

For a river of such stern reputation, the cut banks of the Pecos overlook a very handsome stream. South of Monahans, its clarity invites an afternoon sitting with a sketchpad and watercolors, or a cane pole and bucket of minnows. Shaded with salt cedar in pale bloom, the river water rolls and pools over sand beds in deepening shades of aquamarine—cool swimming holes, surely, and safe enough to fill an empty canteen. But the Highway 18 bridge is only a few miles from the site of the infamous Horsehead Crossing. Comanches used that fording point en route to raid Mexican villages in Chihuahua, and drovers pushed herds of longhorns across it on the nineteenth century trail drives. The name was said to have come from a herd of horses that the Indians drove too hard; sixty miles from their last water, the horses ran into the Pecos and poisoned themselves, drinking its brine. Then, to mark the Pecos crossing, cowboys festooned the mesquites with the horses' skulls.

The Pecos begins as a rowdy mountain creek in the Sangre de Cristos east of Santa Fe, New Mexico, but upstream dams and irrigation have diminished the river's flow. Time may have also lightened the load of bitter salts that the Pecos carries from the desert plains and deposits in Lake Amistad, which backs up through the dramatic rock canyons of its confluence with the Rio Grande. The reminiscences of old-timers suggest it has. But the drovers hated the implications of Horsehead Crossing as much as the hazards of the swim and the taste of the water.

Floral stalks of century plant seem to implore the desert sky.

Previous pages: An archipelago of mountain ranges rises from the desert floor.

203

The beautiful red flowers of the strawberry cactus, or pitaya, are followed by red, succulent fruits that taste deliciously like strawberries when ripe.

Opposite page:
In the vast expanses of the Big Bend country, soaptree yucca often rises to a height of fifteen feet or more.

In Texas, few boundaries mark terrain as emphatically as the Pecos River. People consider themselves West Texans in Fort Worth, 350 miles east of the Pecos. Mesquite trees, midgrasses, and a huge and dusty sky determine the visual effect of intervening ranch country. But even as the rainfall diminishes and the horizons stretch out, the eye finds oaks, junipers, and spring-fed streams—reminders of the benevolent Cross Timbers, Hill Country, and Edwards Plateau. To see these west of the Pecos, you have to get past the thorns and the alkali flats. You have to climb.

⚜

Spaniards simply called it the wilderness, *El Despoblado*. Soaptree yuccas look like an advancing infantry clad in furs and wild spiked helmets. Desert willows line the dry arroyos. In tens and twenties of years but not centuries, the agaves—or century plants—send up spear-shaped flower stalks, then die. The region's prettiest red flowers bloom on fiercely spined clumps called strawberry cactus, or pitaya, and claret-cup cactus. Nowadays, the eye follows an eerily straight, dwindling line of telephone poles to the horizon. Passing the time, you can almost count the boxcars of a slowly moving railroad train; and later realize, crossing the tracks, that you have since driven fifteen miles. Automobiles, and their mechanical condition, seem far more important out here. Water and gasoline cans are seen wired to natives' bumpers. The closest grocery store may be sixty miles away. Residents speak nonchalantly of six-hour drives.

An archipelago of mountain ranges, more than a dozen of them, ascend stark and violet from earth that looks like an endless brown skillet. Peaks in three of those ranges—the Guadalupe, Davis, and Chisos—exceed altitudes of 7,000 feet. But the Trans-Pecos is a northern extension of Mexico's Chihuahuan Desert, and even in the forests of the highest mountains, annual precipitation averages only 10–19 inches. On the desert floor, the rain plays out westward, leaving El Paso with eight inches and a bone-dry evaporation rate. Plants and animals have to accept the terms of this hostile environment. In the crusty dunes of the far west Hueco Basin—typical of the state's remaining share of its public lands—rattlesnakes spend hot summer days burrowed in the scant shade of diminutive mesquites. Their angular heads sit camouflaged on the sand.

Glare intensifies the heat. Some desert plants pursue moisture with large and venturing root systems; succulents make the best of the infrequent rain. In the evolutionary process, the stem tissues of cactus turned into columns or balls of stored water. To avoid losing that reservoir to the evaporation rate, it gave up its leaf system. The bristling spines provide a refractory kind of shade and keep thirsty animals away. The

PHOTO: GEYATA AJILVSGI

Tansy-aster, also known as tahoka daisy, blooms profusely all summer and fall, turning roadsides and abandoned areas into glorious masses of purple.

Previous pages:

The Trans-Pecos is a northern extension of Mexico's Chihuahuan Desert. The Chisos Mountains of Big Bend get only 10–12 inches of rain a year.

flower opens briefly for pollinating insects, hummingbirds, and bats. Most species flower during the harshest daytime heat. Fewer hungry creatures browse the desert then. The young fruit protects itself with more spines or wool. When the seeds mature, the fruit takes on a brighter hue and sweeter taste. Finally, the enemies are encouraged to come and eat.

Deserts bloom with surprising color and variety. Of roughly 5,400 native Texas plants, 2,000 appear in the Trans-Pecos. But man has not treated this surface kindly. Scattered pastures, mostly root-plowed and sown with exotic grasses, hint at the former wealth of its virgin prairie. More sections are grayed in winter by tarbush, mesquite, tumbleweed, and creosote bush, which smells strong and heady after a rain. Creosote bush asserts itself when short-grass prairie declines; it survives overgrazing because herbivores cannot stand the taste of it. Worse than the grazing, far too many hooves trampled the native grasses. Thin topsoil was stripped down to the underlying rocks. And once creosote bush takes over, toxins in the root systems block out competing shrubs and grasses. Trying to make the bleak real estate pay, farmers have planted cotton, cantaloupes, pecan trees, and recently, wine grapes. One of the planet's richest mineral deposits has created cities and endowed their economy, but when flown over, the blackened spots around the pump units and drilling sites add barren meaning to the expression "oil patch."

Monahans Sandhills State Park opens a window into a less disrupted desert floor. Plants that could adapt to an environment of shifting soil did not much suit the palates of the herbivores; the sand hills escaped the intensive ranching. Blowing from the south, the insistent Chihuahuan wind shoves the naked dunes along. Blinding white in the sunshine, yet shadowed with graceful patterns of bluish gray, the sand piles up in ridges and spills over. It has turned up fossils of extinct camels and mastodons. Active dunes change into stationary hummocks when the balance shifts to stabilizing plants: plains yucca, bull nettle, rabbit-brush, prickly pear with tunas that look like pared radishes, and tasajillo cactus, whose bright red berries feed the quail. Beneath the small shinnery oaks, root systems sometimes drill seventy feet.

Not far below the surface, the sand is wet. Water pools in small basins after a thunderstorm. If the storm passes at sunset, the atmospheric moisture and last rays of departing light can create a scenic phenomenon called red rain. As long as the little water hole lasts, mourning doves murmur and wet their wings. On top of the dunes, mounds of bindweed heliotrope bloom white just after the rain. The freshened breeze stirs the scent of sweet sand-verbena. Purple tansy-asters line the park roads. Pink sand-palafoxia and long-stemmed plains sunflowers help hold the deeper soil. Though it's impossible to get lost in the fenced park, a stroll

*P*lains yucca sinks its roots deep into the sand,
the small colonies becoming temporary anchors for
the dunes, which are shoved along by the insistent
Chihuahuan wind. As the sand piles up in ridges
and spills over, it sometimes half-buries the
sparsely scattered plants.

From among desolate brushlands of the mountainous west, lechuguilla raises to the sky tall, slender spikes of reddish purple.

The Guadalupes' majestic El Capitan, Texas's second highest peak, looms above gypsum waste and gleaming salt flats.

Opposite page:
Roselike flowers of snowy white cover shrubby plants of Apache plume during summer. The plant gets its common name from the appearance of its seed heads, which bear beautiful, silky-pink plumes.

through these dunes provokes a certain anxiety. They look too much alike. To the northwest, they go on like this for two hundred miles.

❧

West of the Pecos, you eventually come upon the remains of an ancient barrier reef, now protected as a U.S. national park. Bounded by gypsum waste and gleaming salt flats, the Guadalupe Mountains are mostly a New Mexico range—the southernmost tip of the Rockies. Shrouded in clouds, covered in snow, but more often a gold rock cathedral in morning sunlight, El Capitan looks across outwash foothills and the desert floor. A hundred miles away, El Paso raises a faint orbish glow on clear nights. El Capitan may be Texas's most photogenic mountain, but it's not quite the highest ground. A few miles to its rear, the summit of Guadalupe Peak stakes that claim at 8,749 feet.

The floor's desolation brush gradually yields to lechuguilla and chino grama. At roughly 5,000 feet, the slopes change into a surprisingly robust prairie of bluestem, grama, and muhly grasses. On the north side of the range, shrubs of desert rose bloom pink and yellow amid the shinnery oaks. Elk venture out in the open to browse the rose-hip fruits. Higher up, the prairie blends into a forest that contains seven more species of oak. Though some of the desert's worst is still fresh in mind, senses turn to the thick spiced smell of piñon pine, the outlandish gnarled bark of an alligator juniper, chokecherries that can be made into an excellent tart wine, and the white flowers and feathery purplish fruit of an evergreen shrub called Apache plume.

Mule deer, once the prey of Mescalero Apaches who ruled the Guadalupes, take their name from the size and shape of their ears.

Chapline columbine, one of the rarest plants of the Guadalupe mountains, thrives along a cool, clear-running stream in McKittrick Canyon.

Mescalero Apaches ruled the Guadalupes until 1869, when cavalry troops from Fort Davis surprised them at a water hole down off the eastern escarpment and destroyed everything they left behind. Before the debacle at Manzanillo Springs, the Apaches had hunted elk and mule deer in the heights for three centuries. In limestone middens, they cooked the hearts of maguey, their namesake mescal agave. With sewing needles made from the hornlike points of the century plant's leaves, they used its fibers for thread; and drank themselves drunk on pulque, its fermented sap.

The same year the Apaches lost their hold on the Guadalupes, Captain Felix McKittrick lent his name to the state's prettiest mountain gorge. Broken into north and south forks, McKittrick Canyon twists between sheer limestone cliffs that are gouged with erosion pockets and studded with oceanic fossils. At some points, an upward gaze at the rim spans 2,800 feet. Stocked in recent years with rainbow trout, McKittrick Creek offers a bouldered trail through the south canyon. Cardinal flowers and arrays of bright red tubular penstemons, called royal beardtongues, bloom along the creek. Three rare wildflowers—Texas valerian, a variety of honeysuckle called the McKittrick snowberry, and yellow Chapline columbine—are found only in the Guadalupes' high, moist canyons. Leaves in the aspen groves clack softly in the breeze and turn lemon yellow in the fall.

*M*cKittrick Canyon, the state's prettiest
mountain gorge, twists between sheer limestone
cliffs that are gouged with erosion pockets and
studded with oceanic fossils.

The Guadalupes contain Texas's most varied highland forest. Alligator juniper is named for the reptile-skin appearance of its gnarled and twisted bark.

Along the creek bottom, the range of trees runs from Arizona cypress and bigtooth maple, with autumn color that rivals the gold, orange, and red panoramas of rural New England, to the sensual smooth-armed Texas madrone, which in banana-colored summer bloom would look at home in a Central American rain forest. Conifers change from the squatty piñons, characteristic of the Rockies' southern foothills and perhaps two hundred years old, to Douglas firs and ponderosa pines that stand as tall as ninety feet. Winter blows hard through the Guadalupes. A tree called the limber pine has adapted well to the barrage of wet Pacific fronts and bitter Arctic northers. It first bathes itself with antifreeze. While the boughs of other trees crack under the weight of freezing rain, oozing sap coats the limber pine's needles and keeps ice from sticking. And when the heavy snow falls, the supple branches shrug, droop, and shake the snowdrifts off.

⚜

A hundred and fifty miles to the southeast, by the highways' indirect route, the treeless parade ground and rock barracks of Fort Davis look like an Old West movie set. Preserved by the National Park Service, the frontier fort recalls the time that the military tested camels as beasts of burden in the arid Southwest. The dromedaries seemed at home in the Chihuahuan Desert—hungry enough, they would even eat creosote bush—but saddle horses and pack mules fared about as well, and were both better-humored and more available. The Civil War shelved the project, leaving a few feral camels to plod the desert plateau. Stationed at Fort Davis, black cavalry troops secured the central Trans-Pecos for settlement during Reconstruction. Apaches and Comanches called them buffalo soldiers, because of their dark woolly hair. A generation removed from slavery, they were among the first American blacks thrust into a competitive and resentful job market. So they enlisted in the Army, which would hire them—a social pattern that carries on today.

The little town of Fort Davis is built along a shallow blue creek shaded by cottonwoods. South across the Marfa plains, wind whips the blonde prairie in gleaming ripples. Herds of pronghorn antelope gallop and cut with raised heads and flashes of white rumps. The houses and rust-red barns of the ranchers sit far back in the floor canyons. Some spreads are sown with exotic grasses. But above 4,000 feet, the native grama prairie approaches a state of climax vegetation—the optimum health and stability that plant communities achieve. At 16–19 inches a year, the Davis Mountains get more rain than the rest of the Trans-Pecos. And in stocking pastures and pumping groundwater with windmills, landowners in the oval region have exercised uncommon restraint.

Behind the fort and town, the slanting pillars of the volcanic range are arranged like giant stacks of artillery shells. On hiking trails and winding

At some points, an upward gaze from McKittrick Canyon spans 2,800 feet.

A quarter of a million Indians once lived in caves and planted crops in the fertile bottoms between the present site of El Paso and the immense rock canyons that make white-water rapids of the Rio Grande.

roads, the bordering Davis Mountains State Park nicely juxtaposes oak and pine forest against the distances of grassland plateau. Bristling succulents supply the brightest floral color: blocky thickets of walking-stick cholla, each a single plant, with claret-cup cactus and strawberry cactus perched on the rocks. Prairie stickleaf blooms in the gravel. Sunflowers find enough soil to root in the crevices of cliffs. Tiny white asters, purple devil's-claw, and large yellow clumps of woolly paper-flower crowd the roadsides. Access to private ranches imparts the surest sense of nature in the Davis Mountains, but on clear days, a seventy-four-mile drive on highways 118 and 166 offers a splendid alternative.

Within the state, no region of comparable size contains more endangered vegetation. Seen through Madera Canyon and behind Sawtooth Mountain, which ascends from the north end of the range like a great outstretched hand, Texas's single most delicate habitat may be 8,382-foot Mount Livermore. The Livermore sandwort, Little Aguja pondweed, and Shinner's tickle-tongue grow only in the Davis Mountains. And yet no region looks healthier. On the southwest curve of the driving loop, the highland forest species yield the slopes to soaptree yucca. The drainage patterns are marked not by the raw and naked gullies you come to expect of Texas terrain—instead by desert willows in rose and purplish, orchidlike bloom.

But the magic of the Davis Mountain country is the sky. The University of Texas did not position McDonald Observatory on the summit of Mount Locke solely because of the altitude, 6,791 feet. Few spots on the planet offer a clearer look at outer space. The atmosphere is so clean that the eye plays tricks on you. A sign on the Marfa highway says Fort Davis, 10 miles. You grip the steering wheel and blink. The cottonwoods and water tower couldn't be more than three miles away. Low and deep in the turquoise sky, a few cumulus clouds have made the day's first appearance. This trick reverses three-dimension. The far clouds look closer than the near horizon.

⚜

A thousand years ago, more than a quarter of a million Indians may have planted corn, squash, beans, and pumpkins in fertile bottoms between the present site of El Paso and the immense rock canyons that make the white-water rapids of the Rio Grande. Beavers built dams on the river. It was a deeper and more consistent stream then, and the climate of the Chinati, Bofecillos, Chisos, Mariscal, and Sierra del Carmen mountain ranges was not so dry. By the early eighteenth century, when Spaniards penetrated the Big Bend region, Apaches had asserted themselves in semipermanent encampments called *rancherías*, though the raiding trail of their Comanche tormentors crossed the river at today's Lajitas. The

*W*alking-stick cholla forms immense, impenetrable, spiny thickets but balances its unpleasantness with clusters of incredibly beautiful flowers.

Following pages:
*W*hen settlers first saw Big Bend, the thorned desert plants shared the terrain with climax prairie. Overstocked and overgrazed ranches weakened and reduced the native grasses.

The low, throaty notes of the cactus wren, usually coming from the depths of some cactus clump, are a common sound of the desert brushland.

Never straying far from an ants' nest, the Texas horned lizard, or "horny toad," lies in wait for a bit of food — preferably an ant — to come wandering by.

Opposite page:
Thick petals of claret-cup cactus become almost translucent in the western sun.

last hostile Mescaleros were defeated in northern Mexico in 1880, and attention turned to incoming railroad construction. Silver and mercury mines showed profits for a time at Shafter, Mariposa, and Terlingua.

Though timber was available in the Chisos Mountains, which peak at 7,836 feet, settlers constructed their dwellings with durable adobe blocks made of soil, water, and prairie grass. Merchants called *zacateros* harvested and sold chino grama for use in adobe brickmaking. Sheds and lean-tos were made from the tough, canelike flower stalks of sotol plants. These mountains get only 10–12 inches of precipitation a year, and virtually all of it falls in the summer (a climatic pattern that showcases wildflowers like dwarf zinnias and plains zinnias, which bloom through the fall.) Still, vegetation was the richest natural resource. J.O. Langford, a Mississippi salesman who headed west in 1909 with hopes of curing his malaria, recalled his exhilaration on first seeing the expanse of ripe prairie and vivid flowers:

Clear up to the rocks of the highest ridges it grew, almost hiding the glistening rimrocks, and down on the slopes and down in the valleys, only the tallest of desert plants stood above it. Looking at it then, it seemed to me there was enough grass growing in the Big Bend country to fatten every horse and cow in the United States.

As late as the 1920s, milk arrived at silver and
mercury mining camps on the backs of burros. Big
Bend has not lost that feel of the edge — the
far outpost.

During the next decade, American civilians were urged to evacuate Big Bend; the Mexican Revolution raged across the river, and General John Pershing roved the Chihuahuan terrain, trying to get his hands on Pancho Villa. Soon afterward, hungry American troops in Europe during the First World War supplied the market and rationale for an increasingly overstocked range. Ironically, the worst damage occurred as governmental agencies converted Big Bend from private ranchland to a public nature preserve. With the first trails laid out by a contingent of Franklin Roosevelt's Civilian Conservation Corps, the state acquired most of the parkland by 1942, but during the two years required to complete transfer of the acreage to the National Park Service, ranchers took full advantage of free grazing rights. Today, some of the brightest concentrations of floral color appear above the ground, in the branches of acacias. Big Bend bluebonnets, a tall and winsome variety, still color the lower range in spring, but they're most often found in the company of sand burrs, not little bluestem and chino grama.

*A*lmost lifeless in appearance, the sparse, wind-whipped branches of ocotillo capture the very essence of the desert. But after a rain, the plant becomes a blazing spectacle, the tip of each slender branch seemingly aflame with dense clusters of goldish red flowers.

As late as the 1920s, milk arrived at the mining camps on the backs of donkeys. Big Bend has not lost that feel of being at the edge—the far outpost. Texas's most rewarding nature trail winds up from the National Park lodge and campground in the Chisos Basin. In a pocket cave of a sand-colored cliff, a mountain lion steps out in the sun, raises its rear haunches, and stretches like a front-yard tabby. It's a strenuous, seven-mile hike. Though the Chisos forest contains fragrant piñons and junipers, oaks make the strongest impression. Slender oak, robust oak, and Chisos Mountains oak are endemic species of these highland groves. But as you arrive at the blustery destination, the desert plant formation suddenly reasserts itself.

The South Rim looks out over the barren Sierra Quemada, or Burned Mountains, and the Rio Grande plain. Beyond that, miles of haze and mystery: Latin America. Buzzards laze on the thermals hundreds of feet below. Prickly pear hangs from the ledge, along with a strange, nastily thorned plant called the ocotillo. Tufts of goldish red flowers bloom at the tips of its thin, wind-whipped branches. Not quite as pessimistic as cactus, the ocotillo can still produce foliage. But the branches leaf out only when it rains.

Narrow-leaved trees of desert willow mark the path of moisture-retaining creeks, draws, and arroyos in the arid reaches of West Texas.

Right:
In its hot, dry habitat, desert willow opens showy sprays of orchidlike blossoms after spring and summer rains.

Yucca and bindweed heliotrope spread across an area of snow-white dunes known as the Monahans Sands, once the floor of a Permian sea.

Right:
Shrubby red sage opens distinctively shaped blossoms in full sun along rocky ledges and slopes.

Contrary to popular belief, it is not rain, per se, that causes cenizo to flower. Rather, high humidity is the factor triggering its flowering, and often the bushy shrub will be covered with color, whether or not it has rained.

A solitary plant of day-primrose struggles for
survival in the unstable Monahans Sands, where
the ever-present wind continually reshapes the
dunes, sometimes half-burying the plants,
sometimes almost exposing the roots.

*I*ndian rush-pea usually grows in scattered
colonies, the spikes of yellow and brown
brightening roadsides and ungrazed areas.

Right:
*B*rushlands glow with a bright golden haze when
the mescat acacia blooms. The intense fragrance of
the flowers carries for long distances, attracting
many insects.

Right:

While in bloom, century plants are a mecca for hummingbirds, bats, butterflies, and many insects, which feed on the bountiful pollen and nectar.

"In tens and twenties of years but not centuries, the agaves — or century plants — send up spear-shaped flower stalks, then die."

*P*lants of claret-cup cactus often have many
flower-laden stems that form striking mounds of
orange-scarlet.

Though it appears to perch precariously on its rocky ledge, a claret-cup cactus actually sinks its moisture-seeking roots deep into the cracks of the stony surface.

*R*ichly textured, violet-blue petals of prairie
spiderwort surround feathery stamens brightly
tipped with yellow.

*A native of Argentina, bird-of-paradise has
escaped cultivation and is now scattered throughout
the western brushland. During spring and summer
the shrubs produce large, terminal clusters of
blossoms with pale yellow petals and long
threadlike red stamens.*

Acknowledgments

I wish to thank Geyata Ajilvsgi for her help and
support on our journey through Texas. Her friendship,
energy and enthusiasm were an inspiration. Her
knowledge and generous assistance have been a vital
contribution to this book.

Leo Meier